PURCHASING AND SUPPLY MANAGEMENT: FUTURE DIRECTIONS AND TRENDS

by
Joseph R. Carter, D.B.A., C.P.M.
Purchasing and Logistics Management Program
Arizona State University

and

Ram Narasimhan, Ph.D.
Eli Broad Graduate School of Management
Michigan State University

AWN

ACKNOWLEDGMENTS •

The Center for Advanced Purchasing Studies and the authors would like to thank the participating companies who responded to the survey instrument used to collect data for this study. Several companies served as case-study sites during the formative stage of the project. We thank these companies for their time and assistance.

The following purchasing executives reviewed the manuscript and provided many helpful suggestions for improving its analysis and presentation. Many thanks to

Stewart L. Beall, C.P.M., Cyprus Amax Minerals Company
Thomas J. Lee, General Mills, Inc.
Sherry J. Schaub, C.P.M., The Quaker Oats Company

Finally, we would like to thank the members of the CAPS staff who have contributed to the completion of this study: Carol L. Ketchum, Assistant Director of Administration and Richard A. Boyle, Ph.D., Assistant Director, for their assistance on the manuscript.

Of course, complete responsibility for the final study rests with the authors of this report

       Joseph, R. Carter, D.B.A., C.P.M.   Ram Narasimhan, Ph.D.

ISBN: 0-945968-24-8
LCCN: 95-71340

CONTENTS •

FIGURES AND APPENDICES •

EXECUTIVE SUMMARY •

What jobs will exist for the purchasing and supply management function in companies in the future? The predictions include the following. The absolute number of jobs within purchasing will decrease, as will the layers of management. Purchasing organizations will adopt flatter forms with less emphasis on hierarchy and less distinction between position. Functional silos will become obsolete. The classical functions of marketing, manufacturing, engineering, purchasing, finance, and personnel will be less important in defining work. More people will take on project work focused on continuous improvement of one kind or another. Fundamental restructuring and reengineering will become a way of life at most companies. The primary focal points will be a new market-driven emphasis on creating value with customers, as well as greatly increased flexibility, a new business-driven attack on global markets, which includes a deployment of information technology, and fundamentally new jobs. Work will become integrated in its orientation. The payoffs will increasingly be made through connections across organizational and company boundaries. Included are customer and supplier alliances, with a general focus on improving the value-added chain. New measurements that focus on strategic directions will be required. Metrics will be developed, similar to the cost of quality metric, that incorporate the most important dimensions of the environment. Similar metrics will be developed to support the new uses of information technology. New people management approaches will be developed. Teamwork will be critical to organizational success. Human resource management will become less of a staff function and more closely integrated with the basic work. Many of these predictions are already a reality.

This report is the summary of the **The Purchasing Futures Research Project**, sponsored by the Center for Advanced Purchasing Studies (CAPS). The project's goal is to develop a vision for what the purchasing function will look like in the next century, including roles, responsibilities, capabilities, and organization. The Purchasing Futures Research Project is an assessment of the current and future practices, concerns, and plans for the purchasing function in business concerns throughout North America. The objectives of the project were to gather and analyze information on the current practices, concerns, and of most importance, the plans of these business units, to improve their operational competitiveness through efficient, effective, and novel purchasing organization and practices. The ultimate goal of the project was not to document various purchasing strategies, but to uncover purchasing and corporate business market trends and synthesize these into strategic organizational propositions for what purchasing and supply management might develop into during the next century.

The framework used in this manuscript encompassed four distinct sections: (1) the Executive Purchasing Roundtables in North America and Europe, (2) the survey data analysis and development of a descriptive model, (3) the corporate case study exploratory analysis, and (4) the Purchasing Futures Symposium held at Michigan State University. Each of these sections yielded unique insights into purchasing and supply management's changing future role in the corporation. The executive summary will present salient points from the roundtables, corporate case studies, and final summary and implications.

THE EXECUTIVE PURCHASING ROUNDTABLES

There were many areas of difference between the North American and European roundtable participants. Some of these differences can be explained by culture, a short-term versus longer-term planning orientation, and varying foci on cost reduction through better information management and effectiveness measures.

It seemed apparent to the investigators that cultural differences was only one factor impacting the difference in future directions reported for both executive purchasing and supply management roundtables. A more significant factor was the size of the firm and rate of evolution of purchasing and supply management. For example, larger firms saw a greater need to increase the technical ability of purchasing and supply management employees than did smaller firms. Also, it was apparent to the investigators that the rate of evolution within the purchasing and supply management and supply management arena was more pronounced in North American industries. Part of this difference can be attributed to the need for European firms to plan for the integration of a common market within the continent. For example, the use of sourcing teams by European firms was predicted to increase dramatically as Europe moves to a common supply and logistics marketplace.

There was a clear sense expressed in North America that better information systems and technology was the route being taken to cost reduction and, ultimately, cost avoidance. The Europeans felt that this demonstrated North America's orientation to short-term planning and gains while they, the Europeans, were more longer-term oriented by stressing effectiveness measures rather than efficiency goals. For example, a European manager stated that "Europe has gotten the message that we are in a long, hard fight, but North America has not gotten the message yet." The investigators do not entirely agree with this statement, but report it here as a basis for understanding the perceptions of each group of managers.

COMPANY CASE STUDIES

The corporate case studies suggested several major trends: higher degree of technical training for purchasing and supply management personnel, closer link with markets and customers, strategic orientation and supply management activities instead of traditional roles, expanded responsibility of purchasing department to include quality engineering and assurance, customer satisfaction, emphasis on total cost of purchases, decision models, and supply base rationalization, increasing strategic role of purchasing and supply management, increasing need for training in leadership and influence skills, integration of information systems with suppliers, development of tools and techniques for partnering with suppliers, and broadening influence of sourcing decisions across the value chain.

In addition, corporate case study data suggest that purchasing and supply management personnel in the future will work "outside" the purchasing department as part of integrated, cross-functional teams, their share of the responsibility for products and customer satisfaction will grow, and as market demands for customization and flexibility increase, the role and importance of purchasing and supply management will change.

When viewed collectively the case studies suggest that the observed trends can be grouped into organizational/structural changes, changes in "skill mix," changes in scope of responsibilities, and change to a market orientation.

SUMMARY AND IMPLICATIONS: 11 PROPOSITIONS

The synthesis of the academic symposium, the Executive Purchasing Roundtables, a broad-based survey instrument, and the corporate case studies resulted in the development of 11 propositions concerning the future of purchasing and supply management.

Proposition 1: The strategic importance of purchasing and supply management will increase in the future. Purchasing and supply management will emerge as a key element of business strategy.

Proposition 2: The strategic "reach" of purchasing and supply management will increase in the future.

Proposition 3: Purchasing and supply management will become management of external operations.

Proposition 4: Strategic alliances with suppliers will increase.

Proposition 5: Purchasing and supply management will play a key role in strategic cost management in firms.

Proposition 6: Verticalization of purchasing and supply management practices in organizations will increase.

Proposition 7: Flattening of purchasing and supply management organizations will continue due to the use of horizontal, self-managed teams.

Proposition 8: Management of the "white space," the space between managerial positions and layers, will become increasingly important for purchasing and supply management executives.

Proposition 9: Purchasing and supply management will increasingly come under the influence of the new paradigm —"the learning organization."

Proposition 10: New realities of purchasing and supply management performance evaluation will emerge.

Proposition 11: Purchasing and supply management will emerge as a core competence of firms.

A framework is provided in the last chapter as an attempt to link the various propositions relating to strategic purchasing and supply management futures to specific trends and the competitive focus of the firm. The investigators hypothesize a possible locus of evolution both for competitive priorities and strategic sourcing trends. In developing this thought pattern, the investigators are implicitly asserting that it is the evolution in the competitive focus of the firm that drives purchasing and supply management trends.

These propositions have broad implications for purchasing and supply management in the future. The implications can be grouped into "future purchasing and supply management organization," "future purchasing and supply management practices," and "future purchasing and supply management education and training" and presented succinctly below:

Future Purchasing and Supply Management Organization

- Flatter purchasing and supply management organization
- Fragmentation (distribution) of functional expertise
- Verticalization of supply chains
- Membership in separate supply chains or key business processes
- Cross-functional team or project orientation

Future Purchasing and Supply Management Practices

- New realities of performance evaluation
- Teams in parallel
- Strategic focus
- Supplier alliances
- Supply chain integration
- Greater reliance on information technology
- Market/customer focus
- Total cost decisions
- Strategic cost management
- Greater internal integration across value chain
- Emphasis on time-based strategies
- Reduction of transaction costs
- Value maximization

Future Purchasing and Supply Management Education and Training

- Broader training to facilitate cross-functional team interaction
- Tele-learning and knowledge exchange
- Performance enhancement systems
- Concurrent learning and job performance

INTRODUCTION •

As United States firms strive toward global competitiveness, the effective management of the supply chain and sourcing has assumed great importance. Supply chain management and sourcing have also become academic fields of considerable interest and relevance. It is anticipated that recent and new developments in sourcing and supply management will play a critical role in the restructuring and restoration of U.S. industries as they attempt to regain their global prominence. The idea of a domestic market and economy has been superseded by the more practical view that our markets and economy are a part of the global economy in which American industries must compete.

It is widely acknowledged by industry leaders that achieving global competitiveness requires effective management of the productive and material resources of the organization. The effectiveness with which this is done affects cost, quality, customer satisfaction, and delivery performance of a firm regardless of its manufacturing or service orientation. These aspects of doing business have become the basis of competition in current markets leading to their characterization as "order winners." Consequently, in their relentless pursuit to achieve sustainable competitive advantage over domestic and international competition, U.S. industries are increasingly viewing purchasing not just as an infrastructural or support function but as a strategic weapon.

For U.S. firms, the emphasis on supply management and preoccupation with purchasing is fairly recent. The importance of the integrating role that purchasing plays in firm-level operations deserves greater attention. The principal motivation for this research project stems from a lack of cohesive information, and the realization that the purchasing function will exert a significant influence over manufacturing operations well into the next century.

In many firms, the movement toward an integrated purchasing and supply management strategy has led to pervasive changes in organizational structure, procurement, and new product development practices, transportation operations, and manufacturing facilities. However, the changes and emerging trends in sourcing and supply management and its impact on manufacturing operations is not well-documented. The integrating role that purchasing plays in a firm's operations deserves greater recognition.

Clearly there is a need to document the changes that are taking place and to understand the implications of these changes so that the benefits of sourcing and supply management can be fully realized. This research report, we hope, begins to fulfill the need. It will document the important ways in which its role is changing, and how it will affect tomorrow's manufacturing environment and competitiveness of firms.

Before defining the specific objectives of the project and the method of conducting the research, we briefly discuss the important role that purchasing plays in industrial competitiveness.

PURCHASING AND INDUSTRIAL COMPETITIVENESS

Restructuring and renewed focus on manufacturing operations are currently viewed as the principal means by which U.S. firms can achieve industrial resurgence. This focus has prompted U.S. firms to examine their organizational structures and to pay attention to those aspects of their manufacturing operations that have the potential to increase competitiveness. Although the terms are overused, competitiveness and reengineering are the driving forces in the efforts of U.S. manufacturing industries.

From studying successful international manufacturing firms, U.S. firms have recognized the strategic importance of manufacturing. Many international firms have made substantial inroads into traditional American industries such as steel, automobiles, consumer electronics, and home appliances. These spectacular gains came at the expense of large U.S. companies. The success of international competition has been attributed to their meticulous attention to manufacturing operations, broadly defined to include sourcing, supply management (the procurement of materials and components, and the management of the flow of these items into the production facility).

There is no commonly accepted definition of manufacturing competitiveness. It is generally agreed that competitiveness refers to a firm's ability to maintain and enhance its market share. Several generic strategies that a firm can employ to compete successfully in the market are:

- Be a low-cost producer (i.e., concentrate on cost reduction);
- Be a high-quality producer (i.e., concentrate on quality);
- Compete through manufacturing flexibility and product differentiation;
- Or, combine these generic strategies.

The relevance of effectively managing the material resources of an organization and its competitive success has been observed by both practitioners and researchers in operations management. This research report focuses on material purchasing and encompasses inbound logistics and several linkages existing between purchasing and other functional areas within the firm.

Purchasing is a boundary-spanning function in that it interacts with other functional areas of the firm in important ways. Consequently, an attempt was made to recognize the critical linkage between purchasing and other functions such as engineering, logistics, and manufacturing throughout the research project.

IMPORTANCE OF THE PURCHASING FUNCTION

Too often, the term purchasing is used in industry to connote the procurement of materials, supplies, and services. In a narrow sense, the day-to-day goals of purchasing involve detecting organizational needs, identifying sources of supply, selecting suppliers, arriving at an appropriate price, issuing the contract, and expediting to ensure proper delivery.

Unfortunately, this unduly narrow view of purchasing relegates it to a purely clerical function. Such a narrow view of purchasing is neither correct nor useful. A broader and more accurate view of the general goals of purchasing would include the following seven items.

1. *Provide an uninterrupted flow of materials and services to the operating system.*
   It is assumed by many that the basic tenet of purchasing is to obtain the proper materials and services in the right quality, in the right quantity, at the right time, at the right price, and from the right source. This is only partly true. Without an assurance of supply, these other "rights" are meaningless. A buyer at General Motors was asked to estimate the percentage of items that he purchased that were custom-designed to meet specific GM needs. His surprising answer was "over 90 percent." If this buyer cannot assure supply, the other factors

of quality, price, source, timeliness, etc. would be irrelevant.

2. *Keep inventory investment at a minimum.*
   The purchasing function "spends" the vast majority of sales revenues in most firms. Buying large quantities secures a discounted price and achieves efficiencies in transportation. However, this buying policy would create large inventories resulting in unacceptably high investment in materials . Such an ordering policy is unacceptable in the 1990s. The purchaser must continually strive to reduce inventories without sacrificing price or service quality.

3. *Maximize Quality.*
   For years, purchasing has been involved in working with suppliers to improve the quality of incoming materials. However, purchasing can also maximize a finished product's perceived quality and customer service. Because of purchasing's unique role in integrating the suppliers' operations into the manufacturing operations of the firm, the function can play a major role in promoting total quality management and assuring customer satisfaction.

4. *Find and develop competent sources of supply.*
   The success of any purchasing function can depend on its ability to locate preferred sources worldwide, analyze their capabilities, and select a supplier partner for a long-term relationship (when appropriate). This may entail a search beyond domestic suppliers to find the "right choice." The goal of purchasing should be to find sources of supply that will give competitive advantage to the firm's finished products. More frequently, such sources are discovered internationally.

5. *Standardize, Standardize, Standardize.*
   For years, many firms believed that custom-designed finished goods required custom-designed parts and materials. The Japanese manufacturers have disproved this theory. A major responsibility of purchasing is to gather and disseminate information on standard, available materials that can do the job better and cheaper than parts designed internally. Ideally, such information should be made available during the design stage of product development.

6. *Purchase materials at the lowest total cost of ownership.*
   The profit-leveraging effect of purchasing throughout the materials management cycle can be significant. Purchasing must consider the total cost of ownership (sometimes referred to as life-cycle costing) in acquisitions. It has been suggested that "price" has been replaced by "quality" as the primary consideration in sourcing. Under the broader

view of total cost of ownership, price will continue to play a central role in sourcing.

7. *Foster interfunctional relationships.*
Purchasing buys little for its own use since it is a staff, not line, function. The function exists solely to meet the needs of other functional areas and customers. In that role, purchasing frequently spans the boundary that separates various functions into departments.

During the last two decades, purchasing has evolved from being viewed as little more than a clerical function to its present status as an integral part of managing the operations of a firm. Similarly, purchasing is more than simply buying. Purchasing is involved in materials and services acquisition, product and process development, capacity planning, and total quality management.

INTERFUNCTIONAL LINKAGES

Purchasing is a boundary-spanning activity. Perhaps purchasing develops a closer working relationship with other departments within the firm than any other. There are clear advantages to be gained from such a close-working relationship. The procurement function contributes directly to the operating results and profitability of a firm. The fact that purchasing is responsible for spending more than 60 percent of a manufacturing firm's sales dollars highlights the profit-enhancing potential of the purchasing function. Every dollar saved in purchasing can become equivalent to an additional dollar of profit.

Purchasing and Marketing

The purchasing function can help marketing by buying materials and services at their lowest total cost so that the firm can maintain a competitive position vis a vis other firms. But, the purchasing function can help marketing in other ways. First, international and domestic countertrade is a neglected area in which marketing and purchasing can work together for competitive advantage. Such countertrade practices can help the firm sell its products in new markets. Second, through its involvement in new product development initiatives with marketing, purchasing can help the firm design and develop a product that meets target costs. Finally, through a close-working relationship with marketing, purchasing can help assure customer satisfaction.

Purchasing and Manufacturing

The purchasing functions interface with manufacturing is most direct and the impact that it has on manufacturing performance is readily felt. Without effective management of this interface, it is difficult for firms to pursue TQM, customer satisfaction, time-based competition, JIT, and other initiatives, which are essential in today's competitive environment. It is critical for these two functions to interface effectively to ensure a smooth, efficient control over the materials acquisition process.

Purchasing and Quality Assurance

There has been a major emphasis by the purchasing function in developing quality assurance programs with suppliers. These programs are closely related to the increase in competition from international products and the widespread introduction of the Just-in-Time (JIT) philosophy of manufacture.

Purchasing has discovered that a supplier quality improvement program can have a significant effect on the prices paid for purchased materials. The idea that a firm should necessarily pay a premium price for high quality is untenable. The highest quality supplier should have a very low-cost structure and support competitively low prices.

An improvement in the quality of purchased materials can also have a major effect on the internal operations of the firm. As the quality of incoming materials increases, the costs of expediting, production control, inspection, material handling, and indirect labor decrease substantially.

A quality assurance department was created at Xerox, reporting to the manager of materials management. The department included source surveillance and receiving inspection activities. As a result of the quality improvement program, 50 percent of all incoming material is supplier certified, eliminating the need for receiving inspection at Xerox. Instead, quality assurance personnel visit suppliers on a weekly to monthly basis, to discuss a variety of improvement and planning topics.

The quality assurance personnel work closely with purchasing and buyers located in engineering and design engineers. The quality assurance personnel join these groups in attending sessions in which topics including materials, processes, and tolerances are discussed. In addition, Xerox has instituted a "forward products procurement program" to involve the suppliers in the early stages of the design of new products. Supplier suggestions on the design of new products have resulted in substantial cost savings through improved ease of manufacturing.

Purchasing and Engineering

A major problem in materials management organizations today is the failure to integrate the purchasing function effectively into the engineering system. In many firms, purchasing is just not involved early in the requirements development process, during the product development stage. Purchasing must be integrated with engineering early on during the requirements-determination phase of product development.

Deciding which materials and components to specify for newly developed products is complicated because of the variety of conflicting demands that must be considered. In the traditional model, engineering concerned itself with design and technology while purchasing concerned itself with acquisition of parts and components for the lowest prices at acceptable quality. These two distinct and separate roles led to conflict and lack of synergy between the two functional areas and also to decisions that were suboptimal and therefore reduced the competitiveness of the firm.

In the traditional model, purchasing's liaison role was viewed as one of communicating suggested product and process changes from suppliers to engineering, and representing suppliers in their requests for deviations from existing product conformance specifications. This mode of interaction between purchasing and engineering is ill-suited for today's competitive environment. Under the new model, purchasing and engineering are working cooperatively in cross-functional teams during the product design phase, working together to achieve better make/buy decisions, instituting commodity team buys, and evaluating suppliers in a joint supplier quality improvement effort.

During new product design, purchasing can provide information to engineering concerning the services, components, and materials the firm may decide to buy. Purchasing can help in establishing price, performance, quality, and reliability targets for the product. It can be a source of information concerning supplier capabilities to meet the objectives of the new design.

With such obvious advantages to linking purchasing and engineering more closely, why hasn't this relationship flourished? There are several reasons why purchasing and engineering haven't been more closely linked, especially during new product design. Many firms have no structured product development process. More specifically, these firms either have not created cross-functional teams or have not empowered those teams effectively. The engineering ethos is to avoid purchasing at all costs and do everything possible to deal directly with suppliers. Finally, beyond the endemic resistance to change found in any organization, a physical separation and resulting lack of communication frequently occurs between purchasing and engineering.

Another way to improve the purchasing and engineering interface is the implementation of a commodity-team buying approach. Each team would include representatives from purchasing, material planning, production control, design engineering, and quality. Each team would be responsible for managing the supply base for a specific commodity class of items. Teams would meet regularly and discuss procurement-related issues such as component or supplier selection. In addition, the teams involve themselves in negotiations, monitor quality performance of suppliers and provide any requisite supplier reviews or training. This approach is used by one of the case study firms described later in the report.

What are the benefits of improving the purchasing and engineering interface? At its most fundamental level, such improved communication will foster the transfer of supply market knowledge to engineers while providing needed technical expertise to purchasing. Also, the idea of "design for manufacturability" will be enhanced, manufacturing costs can be reduced, and the time to market for new product introductions should be shortened.

There are several ways to set up this closer relationship. Some companies have used the idea of co-location, that is, placing purchasing staff near to or within engineering or vice versa. Other firms have attempted to hire purchasing employees with technical backgrounds.

A very productive approach used by some firms has been the use of project teams to develop and introduce new products or at least the application of formal reviews of all new designs by a cross-functional team that includes purchasing. Finally, some companies have hired "procurement engineers" who work with design engineers to supply information on the commercial implications of different design approaches.

PROCUREMENT ACTIVITIES AND MAGNITUDE

During the execution of this research project, the role of purchasing was viewed broadly. The purchasing cycle includes all of the activities involved in the buying of materials and services from the time of recognition of need until the product completes its intended useful life. Types of activities, tasks, and functions on a broad scale include:

- Sourcing: Strategic planning, location sources of supply, assuring continuity of supply, reducing risk of supply disruptions, gathering information about supply markets.

- Purchasing Decision Making: Make or buy, standards, supplier certification, value analysis, scheduling, order releasing, budgeting, supplier capacity planning, and supplier control.

- Contracting: Source selections, soliciting bids, cost-price analysis, negotiations, establishing relationships with suppliers, evaluating supplier performance.

- Inventory Management: Transportation, receiving, lot size determination, purchased inventory control, material handling, scrap disposal, materials return.

Every business and service establishment must purchase. Naturally, there is a wide divergence of the types, sizes, and quantities of materials and services purchased by various segments of the economy. Irrespective of the divergence and complexity, competitive demands placed upon business enterprise mandate that the purchasing process be accomplished in a timely and efficient manner.

American industries and governments purchase materials and services costing trillions of dollars annually. The obvious size of these expenditures emphasizes the importance to the economy of the procurement function.

Has there been a failure by American industry to recognize the importance of purchases as a major cost element of business operations? Some would say yes. A review of nearly all operations management journals shows that, historically, management has directed an inordinate amount of attention to the reduction of labor costs. The dollar magnitude of purchases in American industry has significant management implications. Management needs to accord purchasing strategic importance.

Management has developed elaborate systems to control minor elements of total cost while ignoring more important cost elements, such as purchases. Purchases are not just an important cost element in some companies nor is their importance restricted to manufacturing industries. **Material and services purchases are the dominant cost element in the vast majority of America's industry.** A competitive strategy based on cost reduction is impossible without the involvement of purchasing.

THE FUTURE OF AMERICAN INDUSTRY

What jobs will exist in companies in the future — not at the very top nor at the very bottom, but between? The predictions include

- The absolute number of jobs within purchasing will decrease, as will the layers of management. Purchasing organizations will adopt flatter forms with less emphasis on hierarchy and less distinction between position.

- Functional silos will become obsolete. The classical functions of marketing, manufacturing, engineering, purchasing, finance, and personnel will be less important in defining work. More people will take on project work focused on continuous improvement of one kind or another.

- Fundamental restructuring and re-engineering will become a way of life at most companies. The primary focal points will be a new market-driven emphasis on creating value with customers, as well as greatly increased flexibility, a new business-driven attack on global markets (which includes a deployment of information technology), and fundamentally new jobs.

- Work will become integrated in its orientation. The payoffs will increasingly be made through connections across organizational and company boundaries. Included are customer and supplier alliances, with a general focus on improving the value-added chain.

- New measurements that focus on strategic directions will be required. Metrics will be developed, similar to the cost of quality metric, which incorporate the most important dimensions of the environment. Similar metrics will be developed to support the new uses of information technology.

- New people management approaches will be developed. Teamwork will be critical to organizational success. Human resource management will become less of a staff function and more closely integrated with the basic work.

Many of these predictions are already a reality.

DESIGN OF THE STUDY •

During the fall of 1993, a project began that could significantly affect the field of purchasing and materials management over the next decade and beyond. This project was called "The Purchasing Futures Project" was sponsored by the Center for Advanced Purchasing Studies (CAPS), and resulted in this research report titled **Purchasing and Supply Management: Future Directions and Trends.** The project's goal was to develop a vision for what the purchasing function will look like in the next century — roles, responsibilities, capabilities, and organization. The original idea came from a list of critical purchasing topics generated by the CAPS Executive Purchasing Roundtable. The Roundtable participants rated this topic as one of the most important issues facing purchasing and materials management in the decade of the 1990s as companies prepare, re-engineer, and redesign their organizations for the next century.

The Purchasing Futures Research Project is an assessment of the current and future practices, concerns, and plans for the purchasing function in businesses throughout North America. The objectives of the project are to gather and analyze information on the current practices, concerns, and of most importance, the plans of these business units, to improve their operational competitiveness through efficient, effective, and novel purchasing organization and practices. The project will provide answers to several questions, including:

1. What supply management strategies and activities will firms' emphasize over the next five years? Why?

2. What can be the role of purchasing in meeting these strategies and carrying out these activities?

It has become apparent that companies are indeed managing through a turbulent era in which global competition is forcing many firms to rethink their approach to purchasing, and to change their plans rapidly. How will the purchasing process operate in the future? What organizational changes will take place within purchasing and why?

The purpose of the Purchasing Futures Research Project is to provide an examination of the common themes that emerge from North American industry as a whole and certain logical subgroups within that environment. This perspective is taken in the hope that it will be of value to managers who want to understand "what others are doing" in the purchasing arena. It is anticipated that it will also be useful to institutions, like the Center for Advanced Purchasing Studies and the National Association of Purchasing Management, which are seeking to advance knowledge in the purchasing field and to train managers within the purchasing profession.

RESEARCH AND ANALYSIS

The research and analysis plan for the Purchasing Futures Research Project encompassed four distinct phases — (Phase I: the Executive Purchasing Roundtables in North America and Europe; Phase II: the survey data analysis and development of a descriptive model; Phase III: the corporate case study exploratory analysis; and Phase IV: the Purchasing Futures Symposium held at Michigan State University). Each of these sections yielded unique insights into purchasing and supply management's changing future role in the corporation.

Phase I

Managing a research project under the auspices of the Center for Advanced Purchasing Studies (CAPS) provided the investigators with a unique opportunity to obtain feedback from two very different groups of purchasing executives. The investigators were asked to gather feedback interactively concerning the purchasing futures project from the participants of the CAPS North American Executive Purchasing Roundtable and the CAPS European Executive Purchasing Roundtable. Each group of executives was asked to respond to various purchasing trend issues through the use of the OptionFinder methodology. The same methodology and questions were used at both Roundtables and comparisons between the two groups proved possible. The interactive real-time assessment allowed the investigators to show the response results to the participants and to gain further insight from their comments.

Phase II

Phase II of the study involved the development of a comprehensive questionnaire (see Appendix A), which was mailed to 2,500 purchasing personnel at all levels within firms spanning several classifications of industry groups. The following chapters of this report contain a more detailed description of this effort.

Results focus on differences between industry sectors. The study team cross-tabulated results by industry classification type and size of firm. Members of the study team have extensive knowledge and experience in rigorous and varied methods of analysis. In addition, all analyses were iterative, allowing the team to test new hypotheses in response to early findings. The study team worked as a group to decide upon additional analyses, so that no single point of view or analytic preference dominated. In this manuscript, the researchers present the fruits of their research journey to date.

Phase III

The investigators performed eight corporate case studies to gauge the validity of the information generated during Phase I of the project and to discuss with industry leaders their view of the changing role of purchasing over the next two decades. The companies selected for the interviews spanned the spectrum of service, retail, manufacturing, and governmental sectors and all were considered leaders in their respective fields. The interviewees at each site were top-level executives in the various functional areas affected by purchasing decision making. The investigators spent at least one full day at each of these companies examining the issues.

Focus group discussions using industry representatives, at the corporate case study field visits, were an integral research tool for this study. The reason for using focus groups is that they have a unique place as a confirmatory method for testing complex models. The principal investigators in this study have extensive experience with focus group research and have published research using this technique. More specifically, the researchers have published articles and monographs in which they used focus groups to test complex models.

Phase IV

Immediately after proposal approval, the principal investigators began planning an academic focus symposium at Michigan State University to discuss with leading-edge theoreticians the changing role of the purchasing profession in the 21st century. This symposium brought together a select group of academics to present papers discussing purchasing's future role in the industrial and governmental sectors. Each of these academics had displayed knowledge on this subject through substantial previous research and/or publications. The printed results of this symposium were compiled by the investigators and published as a separate section of this research report. This symposium allowed the investigators to develop a sense of understanding about strategic directions for purchasing and materials management that facilitated the broad-based synthesis and interpretation of future trends. The papers presented at the Purchasing Futures Symposium are provided in Appendix D.

Objectives

The objectives for this manuscript can be stated simply:

- To convey the sense of importance the researchers feel about purchasing's future role in firms' performance.

- To examine the issues that surround purchasing's role.

- To offer a framework that managers can use to understand purchasing's future role.

- To offer some specific advice to purchasing personnel concerning their role.

To fulfill these objectives, the investigators pursued a very rigorous research strategy, consisting of sophisticated, multivariate statistical methods of analysis. The objective in the presentation of these methodologies is not to confuse the practitioner, but to demonstrate to the practitioner and academic alike that good research techniques and design were used in arriving at the results and conclusions presented in this report. The researchers feel the results reported have scientific and practical significance.

THE EXECUTIVE PURCHASING ROUNDTABLES •

Managing a research project under the auspices of the Center for Advanced Purchasing Studies (CAPS) provided the investigators with a unique opportunity to obtain feedback from two very different groups of purchasing executives. The investigators were asked to gather feedback interactively concerning the purchasing futures project from the participants of the CAPS North American Executive Purchasing Roundtable and the CAPS European Executive Purchasing Roundtable. Each group of executives were asked to respond to survey question 12 (see Appendix A) through the use of the OptionFinder methodology. The same methodology and questions were used at both Roundtables and comparisons between the two groups proved interesting. The interactive real-time assessment allowed the investigators to show the response results to the participants and to gain further insight from their comments. This section provides the results of these interactive assessments from both roundtables and the investigators' explanations and interpretations of these responses.

The 1994 North American Executive Purchasing Roundtable

The North American Executive Purchasing Roundtable was held in Phoenix, Arizona, during late February 1994. There were 75 executive participants at the Roundtable. A listing of the enterprises involved in the conference are provided in Figure 1. Seventeen of the 69 enterprises listed in Figure 1, 24.63 percent, were nonmanufacturing enterprises, with the remaining 75.37 percent representing manufacturing concerns. Figure 2 provided a listing of the 36 scale items surveyed, the number of respondents for each item, the average response score, and the diversity index for the item. The number of respondents for each scale item was less than the total number of Roundtable participants. If a respondent had never used a particular activity and had no intention of emphasizing that activity in the future, the respondent was instructed not to input a response for that item.

Another interesting measure provided in the figures in this chapter is called the "Diversity" index. The "Diversity" index is based on a common statistical calculation. It is calculated as the sum of the squared deviations from the mean, average, (Sum of Squares) that exist across respondents for each scale item divided by the maximum Sum of Squares that exist given the 7-point Likert scale used in the questionnaire. Thus, the

index is the proportion of diversity that does exist in the responses relative to what could exist. "Diversity" index scores around zero (0) indicate that all respondents voted nearly the same way, scores around one-hundred (100) mean that participants are "clustered" around both ends of the measurement scale (e.g., one-half responded as low as possible and one-half responded as high as possible), and scores around fifty (50) can be interpreted as responses being scattered across all possible scale values, with no clusters at all. The diversity indexes for all scale items are equal to or less than 25. This indicates that the participants, irrespective of industry group, were mainly in agreement on each scale-item response.

Figure 3 provides a listing of the five "most significant" purchasing and supply management trends identified by the 1994 North American Executive Purchasing Roundtable participants. There are several interesting implications in these responses. First, there is a clear indication of greater strategic importance being placed upon purchasing and supply management decisions. The increased emphasis to be placed on strategic supplier alliances (mean response = 6.0) and strategic sourcing (mean response = 5.9) demonstrates that strategic rather than tactical decisions will weigh heavily within purchasing over the next five years. Also, these responses indicated that purchasing and supply management decisions are expected to have a greater strategic impact on firm performance in the future. Second, there will be a greater reliance placed upon information use (mean response = 6.2) and information technology/EDI (mean response = 5.9) to support purchasing and supply management decision making over the next five years. Finally, the purchasing and supply management function will move further away from clerical-oriented to a more planning-oriented function/TCO (mean response = 6.0) in the near future. In sum, there was general agreement between the respondents - note the very low diversity indexes - that purchasing will play a much greater role within the firm over the next five years and beyond.

Figure 4 provides a listing of the four least significant purchasing and supply management trends identified by the 1994 North American Executive Purchasing Roundtable participants. Again, there are several interesting implications in these responses. First, in the overall listing of responses, Figure 2, time-based purchasing strategies was rated fairly high, mean response of 5.5. Can time-based purchasing strategies be pursued with-

FIGURE 1
1994 NORTH AMERICAN EXECUTIVE PURCHASING ROUNDTABLE PARTICIPANTS

Carnival Cruise Lines	United Technologies Corp.
Pemex	Land O'Lakes, Inc.
The First National Bank of Chicago	Deere & Co.
National Association of Purchasing Management	American Express
Cyprus Amax Minerals Company	Ameritech
Italtel	BellSouth Telecommunications, Inc.
Boeing	Honeywell, Inc.
The Upjohn Company	Exxon Co., USA
Northern Telecom Ltd.	Thomson Consumer Electronics
Pitney Bowes, Inc.	Asea Brown Boveri
Sematech	Drake University
Purchasing Management Association of Canada	The Dial Corp.
Federal Express Corp.	Mobil Oil Corp.
Amoco Corp.	US West Business Resources
The Pillsbury Company	General Mills, Inc.
General Electric Corp.	Lockheed Corp.
AT&T	National Minority Supplier Development Council
Bell Canada	Lederle Laboratories
Martin Marietta Corp.	Miller/Bevco
Unisys Corp.	Bechtel Corp.
American Airlines	Bellcore
Eastman Kodak Company	Caterpillar, Inc.
Bell Atlantic	Conoco, Inc.
Nevie	Texaco, Inc.
Hughes Aircraft Co.	Coca-Cola USA
The M.W. Kellogg Co.	The Quaker Oats Company
BP Oil Co.	Texas Instruments, Inc.
Burlington Northern Railroad	Scientific Atlanta
Westinghouse Electric Corp.	Miles, Inc.
Bank of America	AlliedSignal, Inc.
Northrop Corp.	Ontario Hydro
Ciba-Geigy Ltd.	Champion International
Shell Oil Co.	Kellogg Co.

FIGURE 2
1994 NORTH AMERICAN EXECUTIVE PURCHASING ROUNDTABLE
DEGREE OF EMPHASIS OVER NEXT FIVE YEARS

	Item	N*	Group Mean	Diversity
a.	Sourcing Teams	69	5.8	13
b.	Co-location	55	4.7	12
c.	Supply-base Reduction	71	5.4	20
d.	Technical Qualif.	73	5.7	13
e.	TQM	74	5.2	19
f.	Strategic Sourcing	72	5.9	13
g.	Purchasing Sys. & Serv.	74	5.5	16
h.	Forecasting	74	5.2	17
i.	Supplier Support	71	5.7	15
j.	Reducing Transaction Costs	73	5.7	20
k.	EDI	70	5.9	15
l.	Supplier Alliances	72	6.0	16
m.	Supply Chain Integration	69	5.6	16
n.	Outsourcing	71	5.6	16
o.	Flattening Purchasing Org.	72	4.8	21
p.	CFTs	69	5.5	18
q.	Purchasing Perf. Measures	73	5.8	13
r.	Just-in-Time	69	5.3	13
s.	Environ. Sensitive Purch.	73	5.6	14
t.	Total Cost	72	6.0	13
u.	Supplier Councils	60	5.1	23
v.	Cooper. Network of Suppliers	64	5.0	15
w.	Global Sourcing	65	5.2	19
x.	Time-based Strategies	68	5.5	16
y.	Strategic Cost Mgt.	73	5.7	15
z.	Emphasis of Pur. & Supply	71	5.5	16
aa.	Cost Avoidance	70	4.6	25
ab.	Pur. Process Reengineering	70	5.7	17
ac.	Int. Pur. & Design	60	5.4	16
ad.	Int. Pur & Logistics	66	5.2	17
ae.	Information Technology	73	6.2	12
af.	Third-party Purchasing	58	4.6	19
ag.	Reducing Pur. Cycle Time	71	5.6	17
ah.	Alliance Purchasing	63	5.3	15
ai.	"World-Class" Benchmarks	70	5.8	15
aj.	Reverse Logistics	73	5.6	14

* If the respondent had never emphasized the activity in the past and had no intention of emphasizing the activity in the future, he/she was instructed not to answer the question.

FIGURE 3
1994 NORTH AMERICAN EXECUTIVE PURCHASING ROUNDTABLE:
PURCHASING/SUPPLY MANAGEMENT MOST SIGNIFICANT TRENDS

Item	N	Group Mean	Diversity
Increased Use of Information Technology	73	6.2	12
TCO for Purchase Decisions	72	6.0	13
Supplier Strategic Alliances	72	6.0	16
Strategic Sourcing	72	5.9	13
EDI	70	5.9	15

FIGURE 4
1994 NORTH AMERICAN EXECUTIVE PURCHASING ROUNDTABLE:
PURCHASING/SUPPLY MANAGEMENT LEAST SIGNIFICANT TRENDS

Item	N	Group Mean	Diversity
Shift from Cost Reduction to Cost Avoidance	70	4.6	25
Third-Party Purchasing	58	4.6	19
Co-location of Suppliers and Buying Firms	55	4.7	12
Flattening the Purchasing Organization	72	4.8	21

out emphasizing co-location of buyer and supplier firms, mean response of 4.7? Second, the emphasis on using total cost for purchasing decisions is predicated on the concept of shifting purchasing focus from one of reducing costs to avoiding costs. Yet, the shift from cost reduction to cost avoidance by purchasing is rated very low, mean response of 4.6: the lowest response. This is an inconsistency that purchasing must address, if it wants to have strategic impact within the firm. Finally, a "quick response" strategy, "time-based competition," the "horizontal corporation," etc., argue for flatter organizations. Why did the respondents rate flattening of the purchasing organization so low, mean response of 4.8? One possible explanation offered by several participants was that they had already expended a great deal of effort on flattening the organization and further efforts in this area are unlikely.

Figure 5 provides a listing of the four "middle-of-the-pack" purchasing and supply management trends identified by the 1994 North American Executive Purchasing Roundtable participants. There were some surprising results in this group. First, quality-related issues, mean response of 5.2, will receive less emphasis over the next five years compared to 26 other issues out of 36 issues. Does this mean that quality is fading in importance for North American industries. The respondents think not, just that the manifestation of quality will change. Over the next five years, quality will be equated with flexibility, mass customization, cycle-time reduction, and other issues. Second, cooperative networks of suppliers, being touted by some as a major competitive strategy with materials management, seems not a major trend, mean response of 5.0. In reflection, the participants felt that this issue was more suited to the service industry than others. Finally, supply chain management, a commonly used buzzword, requires a close interaction between purchasing and logistics. Yet these two issues were not rated highly by the Roundtable participants. The general sense was that the issue of supply chain management, although important, was easier said than done, and this would not be a driving impetus for purchasing and supply management over the next five years.

The 1994 European Executive Purchasing Roundtable

The first European Executive Purchasing Roundtable was held in Amsterdam, The Netherlands, during early October 1994. There were 45 executive participants at the roundtable. Figure 6 provides a listing of the 36 scale items surveyed, the number of respondents for each item, the average response score, and the diversity index (representing the level of agreement/disagreement among responses) for the item. Once again, the number of respondents for each scale item was less than the total number of Roundtable participants. If a respondent had never used a particular activity and had no intention of emphasizing that activity in the future, the respondent was instructed not to input a response for that item. Note that the diversity indexes for all scale items were significantly higher for the European respondents than for the North American respondents. Clearly, there was a much higher diversity of opinion on the future directions of purchasing and supply management within Europe.

Figure 7 provides a listing of the six "most significant" purchasing and supply management trends identified by the 1994 European Executive Purchasing Roundtable participants. There are several interesting implications in these responses. First, the use of sourcing teams, mean response of 5.7, and TQM, mean response of 5.4, are strategies that have been emphasized in North America for several years but seem to be only now becoming strong future directions for European purchasing and supply management functions. Oddly, the European participants felt strongly that their purchasing function was further developed and more sophisticated than that of their North American counterparts — clearly an area of disagreement. Second, the Europeans intend to emphasize environmentally sensitive "green" purchasing far more extensively than the North American participants. This is logical given the European fixation on recycling and reuse of materials. Perhaps this is an issue we should rethink in North American purchasing and supply management. Third, sourcing issues come out strongly in the European responses because of the integration caused by the emerging common market. It was felt that the new common market will require much restructuring of sourcing pat-

FIGURE 5
1994 NORTH AMERICAN EXECUTIVE PURCHASING ROUNDTABLE:
PURCHASING/SUPPLY MANAGEMENT MIDDLE OF THE PACK

Item	N	Group Mean	Diversity
TQM	74	5.2	19
Cooperative Network of Suppliers	64	5.0	15
Integration of Purchasing and Logistics	69	5.6	16
Supply Chain Integration	66	5.2	17

23

FIGURE 6
1994 EUROPEAN EXECUTIVE PURCHASING ROUNDTABLE:
DEGREE OF EMPHASIS OVER NEXT FIVE YEARS

	Item	N*	Group Mean	Diversity
a.	Sourcing Teams	38	5.7	21
b.	Co-location	37	3.8	36
c.	Supply-base Reduction	43	5.3	31
d.	Technical Qualif.	43	5.5	23
e.	TQM	42	5.4	16
f.	Strategic Sourcing	42	5.7	17
g.	Purchasing Sys. & Serv.	42	5.2	14
h.	Forecasting	39	4.9	24
i.	Supplier Support	41	5.3	21
j.	Reducing Transaction Costs	43	5.1	31
k.	EDI	43	5.1	23
l.	Supplier Alliances	43	5.1	20
m.	Supply Chain Integration	42	5.0	30
n.	Outsourcing	43	4.9	20
o.	Flattening Purchasing Org.	44	4.5	32
p.	CFTs	42	5.1	21
q.	Purchasing Perf. Measures	43	5.2	32
r.	Just-in-Time	43	4.3	20
s.	Environ. Sensitive Purch.	44	5.4	19
t.	Total Cost	44	5.6	12
u.	Supplier Councils	35	3.0	30
v.	Cooper. Network of Suppliers	36	3.6	30
w.	Global Sourcing	41	5.1	28
x.	Time-based Strategies	39	4.7	29
y.	Strategic Cost Mgt.	43	5.2	29
z.	Emphasis of Pur. & Supply	42	4.7	26
aa.	Cost Avoidance	39	4.6	21
ab.	Pur. Process Reengineering	42	5.1	26
ac.	Int. Pur. & Design	40	4.8	33
ad.	Int. Pur & Logistics	41	4.5	33
ae.	Information Technology	43	5.2	20
af.	Third-party Purchasing	41	3.6	38
ag.	Reducing Pur. Cycle Time	43	4.3	23
ah.	Alliance Purchasing	36	3.9	28
ai.	"World-Class" Benchmarks	42	5.1	34
aj.	Reverse Logistics	33	3.2	42

* If the respondent had never emphasized the activity in the past and had no intention of emphasizing the activity in the future, he/she was instructed not to answer the question.

FIGURE 7
1994 EUROPEAN EXECUTIVE PURCHASING ROUNDTABLE:
PURCHASING/SUPPLY MANAGEMENT MOST SIGNIFICANT TRENDS

Item	N	Group Mean	Diversity
Use of Sourcing Teams	38	5.7	21
Strategic Sourcing	42	5.7	17
TCO for Purchase Decisions	44	5.6	12
Increasing Technical Quality for Purchasing Employees	43	5.5	23
Environmentally Sensitive Purchasing	44	5.4	19
TQM	42	5.4	16

FIGURE 8
1994 EUROPEAN EXECUTIVE PURCHASING ROUNDTABLE:
PURCHASING/SUPPLY MANAGEMENT LEAST SIGNIFICANT TRENDS

Item	N	Group Mean	Diversity
Supplier Councils	35	3.0	30
Reverse Logistics	33	3.2	42
Cooperative Network of Suppliers	36	3.6	30
Third-Party Purchasing	41	3.6	38
Co-Location of Buyer & Supplier Firms	37	3.8	36
Alliance Purchasing	36	3.9	28

terns. Finally, many of the other issues ranked highly by the European group were also ranked highly by the North American respondents. In the areas of emphasis, there is more commonality than dissension.

Figure 8 provides a listing of the six "least significant" purchasing and supply management trends identified by the 1994 European Executive Purchasing Roundtable participants. Several implications and comparisons can be made from these results. First, two trends that were "least significant" for North American respondents were also to be less emphasized by the European participants. Third-party purchasing, mean response of 3.6, and co-location of buying and supplier firms, mean response of 3.8, were rated at the bottom for both groups of participants. There seems to be general agreement that these two issues will be "non-issues" over the next five years. Second, the Europeans seem to be focused on more traditional purchasing practices and less on innovative practices that bring the supply chain together for common leverage. For example, the Europeans rated several supply base initiatives low. The use of supplier councils, mean response of 3.0 (the lowest rating), cooperative networks of suppliers, mean response of 3.6, and alliance purchasing, mean response of 3.9, all require both a horizontal and vertical integration and management of the supply chain. Europeans seem to be maintaining an internal focus to purchasing and supply management. Finally, the diversity indexes for the European "least significant" purchasing and supply management trends were significantly higher than those of their North American counterparts and significantly highly than the indexes for their own "most significant" trends. There is clearly much agreement about what to emphasize over the next five years but significantly less agreement about what to de-emphasize.

In summary, there are many areas of difference between the North American and European roundtable participants. Some of these differences can be explained by culture, a short-term versus longer-term planning orientation, and varying foci on cost reduction through better information management and effectiveness measures.

PURCHASING AND SUPPLY MANAGEMENT: FUTURE DIRECTIONS AND TRENDS •

The discussion of the results in this section parallels the discussion of the statistical methodology provided in a previous chapter. While we realize that the nonacademic reader might not wish to peruse the details, we have chosen to present a fairly comprehensive discussion of the results of statistical analysis for the sake of establishing rigor and completeness of documentation. To the best of our ability, the investigators have tried to balance the various needs of both academics and practitioners.

The data were collected using a mail survey. Two thousand five hundred (2,500) surveys were mailed to a stratified random sample of NAPM and CAPS members. A complete copy of the questionnaire is contained in Appendix A. A "Glossary of Terms" was sent with each questionnaire and is reprinted in Appendix B. The cover letter enclosed with each questionnaire is included in Appendix C. Of the 2,500 surveys that were sent, 361 were returned for a response rate of 14.4 percent. The data were input using Paradox for Windows on an IBM compatible personal computer. The data was then transferred to another PC where statistical analysis was performed using SPSS for Windows and SAS for Windows.

THE RESPONDENTS

The examination of the data started with an analysis of the respondents. From the numerous classification questions, an overall picture of the respondents was formed. Using the three-digit Standard Industry Code (SIC), respondents were grouped into manufacturing and nonmanufacturing categories. An exhaustive analysis of industry groups by SIC classification was not possible given the size of the sample. Figure 9 shows that 62.12 percent of the responses were from manufacturing and 37.88 percent were from nonmanufacturing industries.

The respondents were asked also to choose a category that best describes the products/markets of their business unit. The options available to the respondents were capital goods, consumer goods, industrial goods, consumer services, and industrial services. Figure 10 shows the results of this categorization. The industrial goods sector accounted for the largest number of respondents at 33.15 percent. The consumer goods category was the second most frequent with 29.53 percent of responses. Capital goods was the third most frequent

FIGURE 9
RESPONDENTS BY INDUSTRIAL SECTOR

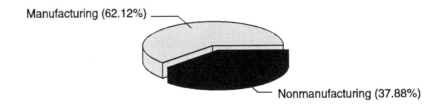

FIGURE 10
RESPONDENTS BY PRODUCT/MARKET

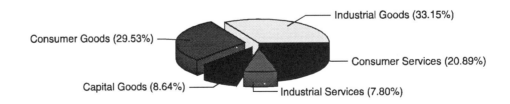

FIGURE 11
RESPONDENTS BY BUSINESS UNIT

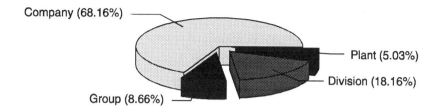

classification with 8.64 percent of the respondents. If these classifications are compared to the Standard Industrial Code (SIC) classifications, there are slightly more respondents classifying themselves into the overall manufactured goods category (71.2 percent) than there are in the SIC manufacturing category (62.1 percent).

Another possible way to look at the distribution of respondents is to examine the type of business unit for which they are reporting. The possible unit types are plant, division, group, or company. The results of this analysis is summarized in Figure 11. More than half of the respondents, 68.16 percent, were reporting from a company-level perspective, 18.16 percent from a division-level perspective, 8.66 percent from a group-level perspective and only 5.03 percent from a plant-level perspective.

Interpretation: *Figures 9,10, and 11 characterize the majority of respondents as being predominantly from manufacturing firms producing either industrial or consumer goods and responding to the questionnaire from a company-level perspective.*

FINANCIAL DATA

The respondents were asked to give the percentage of domestic versus international sales for their business unit. A chart of the responses is shown in Figure 12. The raw data showed that, on average, 83.99 percent of sales for the respondents' business units were domestic, and 16.01 percent, on average, were international.

But, averages frequently don't tell the entire story. In order to compare the domestic mix of the business units to other measures, a cluster analysis was performed on the survey respondents. A cluster analysis is a statistical procedure that places the respondents into logically similar groups based upon their individual responses to a particular question. As a result of the cluster analysis, three distinctive groups of respondent categories were identified based on their International/domestic sales mix. Those categories were Mostly Domestic sales, Mixed Domestic/International sales, and Mostly International sales.

Figure 13 presents the outcome of the classification. The mostly domestic group has the highest percentage of respondents (71.47 percent), mixed is the second largest group classification with 24.23 percent of respondents, while the mostly international group accounts for only 4.29 percent of the respondents.

Interpretation: *Clearly, the vast majority of respondents characterize themselves as primarily domestic operations oriented.*

FIGURE 12
BUSINESS UNIT SALES BY INTERNATIONAL/DOMESTIC MIX

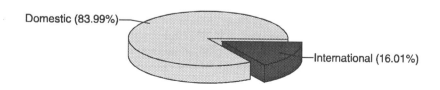

FIGURE 13
RESPONDENTS BY INTERNATIONAL/DOMESTIC

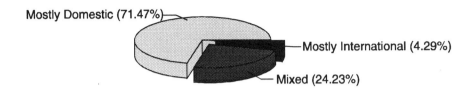

FIGURE 14
MEAN SALES OF THE BUSINESS UNIT

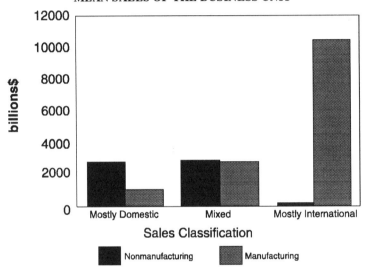

Figure 14 shows the data on the sales of the business unit (mean equals $2.031 billion) for both industry groupings, manufacturing and nonmanufacturing, segmented by sales classification. **Interpretation:** *Respondents from manufacturing firms with significant international operations had much higher average sales than nonmanufacturing firms and firms with mostly domestic or mixed operations.*

Figure 15 presents the overall net profit before tax as a percent of sales for the respondent business units. The mean net profit before tax as a percent of sales for the entire sample equaled 9.12 percent, but this does not tell the complete story. Across all international/domestic sales groups, nonmanufacturing firms had a higher overall net profit before taxes than did their manufacturing counterparts.

Figure 16 depicts the average annual growth rate of sales over the past three years for the respondents. The average growth rate of sales for all respondents equals 11.91 percent with only a slight difference between manufacturing and nonmanufacturing industries. Firms with a mostly international sales focus had a significantly higher annual growth rate than did firms with mostly domestic or mixed sales.

Figure 17 depicts the average return on sales (ROS) over the last three years for the respondent groupings. The overall average ROS mean equals 9.799 percent. For each sales grouping, nonmanufacturing firms had a higher ROS than manufacturing firms. Also, firms with mostly domestic operations and mixed operations had a higher ROS than firms with mostly international operations.

Summary: All four categories of success — sales, net profit as a percent of sales, growth rate of sales, and return on sales (ROS) — were compared by the domestic/international mix of sales and whether the respondents were from manufacturing or nonmanufacturing industries. It is interesting to note that the mostly international manufacturing sector has the highest overall average sales figure ($10.275 billion), while the mostly

FIGURE 15
MEAN NET PROFIT BEFORE TAX AS A PERCENT OF SALES

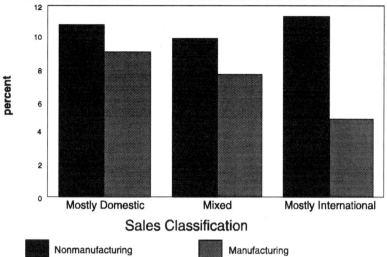

FIGURE 16
AVERAGE ANNUAL GROWTH RATE OF SALES OVER THE LAST THREE YEARS

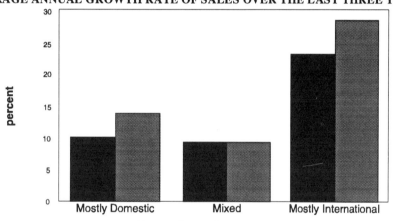

FIGURE 17
AVERAGE RETURN ON SALES OVER THE LAST THREE YEARS

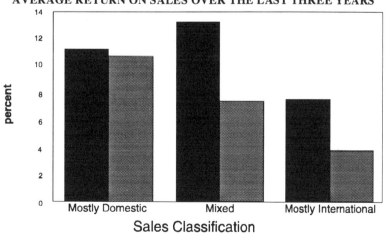

domestic manufacturing has the lowest average sales figure ($.912 billion). This can be contrasted with the average net profit before tax for the two groups, manufacturing and nonmanufacturing. In this case, the average net profit for the mostly domestic manufacturing sector is 8.9 percent, while the mostly international manufacturing sector is considerably lower at 4.8 percent. Also, in every sales mix category, the nonmanufacturing sector has a higher average net profit than the manufacturing sector. In examining the average annual growth rate of sales for the past three years, the international segment has the greatest growth rate, 28.21 percent for manufacturing firms and 22.8 percent for nonmanufacturing firms. This is again contrasted with the average return on sales (ROS) for the past three years. The highest average ROS for the manufacturing sector is for the mixed (domestic and international sales) category with 12.96 percent ROS, while the lowest average ROS is for the mostly international manufacturing sector with 7.25 percent ROS.

Interpretation: *The questionnaire respondents are from medium to large size, relatively successful and profitable firms. Clearly, respondents with predominantly international operations were larger, growing faster, but slightly less profitable than domestic sales-oriented firms. This supports the conventional wisdom that global markets are growing faster than the domestic market, but the level of competition in the global arena is intense, thereby constraining average return on sales.*

A FINAL ANALYSIS OF RESPONDENTS

A cluster analysis was performed on the responses for the average ROS of respondent firms, the net profit before taxes as a percentage of sales, and the level of customer satisfaction. The purpose of this analysis was to further uncover any similarities among and between the respondents to the questionnaire. Hopefully this analysis would provide further insight into the character of the responses. The respondents were categorized into three clusters groupings: low, average, and high.

Figures 18 through 20 show the final cluster groups, along with a chart showing the percentage of respondents that fall into each cluster.

Interpretation: *This methodology characterized the respondents to the questionnaire as large, profitable firms that view themselves as providing an average-or-above level of customer satisfaction. These are important facts to keep in mind during the analysis of purchasing futures; that is, these are the suggested futures of very successful firms and not laggards.*

**FIGURE 18
NUMBER OF CASES:
RETURN ON SALES CLUSTER**

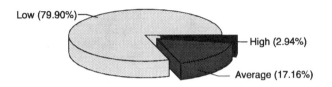

**FIGURE 19
NUMBER OF CASES IN NET PROFIT CLUSTERS**

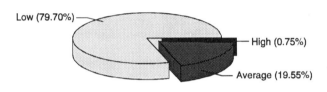

**FIGURE 20
NUMBER OF CASES: CUSTOMER SATISFACTION**

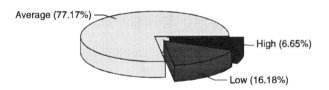

STRATEGY OF THE BUSINESS UNIT

The respondents were asked to indicate the degree of importance to be placed by their business unit on 12 strategic priorities over the next five years (see survey question 11 in Appendix A). The investigators hypothesized that future directions of purchasing might be different depending upon what competitive strategy the business unit intended to stress in the future, over the next five years. Therefore, this question sought to uncover these future business unit strategic priorities. The

FIGURE 21
STRATEGIC PRIORITIES

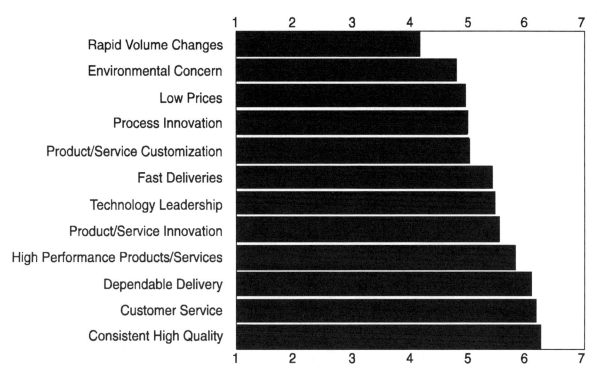

Average Rating Score

respondents were asked to evaluate each of the 12 priorities on a seven-point scale anchored on one end (1) by the term "Of Little or No Future Importance" and on the other end (7) by the phrase "Of Critical Future Importance."

Figure 21 shows a summary of the responses according to the degree of importance of a list of potential competitive factors to the business unit in competing successfully over the next five years.

Future Strategic Priority	Average Rating Score
(1) Consistently High Quality	6.18
(2) Customer Service	6.10
(3) Dependable Delivery	5.99
(4) High Performance Products/Services	5.73
(5) Product/Service Innovation	5.47
(6) Technology Leadership	5.36
(7) Fast Deliveries	5.33
(8) Product/Service Customization	4.96
(9) Process Innovation	4.93
(10) Low Prices	4.86
(11) Environmental Concerns	4.72
(12) Rapid Volume Changes	4.09

As you can see from the list of strategic priorities and mean rating scores, the three competitive factors with the highest overall mean score in descending order of importance are (1) high quality, (2) customer service,

and (3) dependable delivery. These findings correspond with several surveys of manufacturers and nonmanufacturers published during the last two years. (See, for example: Monczka, R.M. and R.J. Trent (1995) *Purchasing and Sourcing Strategy: Trends and Implications*, Tempe, AZ: Center for Advanced Purchasing Studies: p. 21).

Interpretation: *Companies will compete in the future predominantly on the factors of quality, customer service, and delivery performance. A high level of customer satisfaction, a bundle of high quality products and services, can moderate the need for low prices. Also, environmentally sensitive manufacturing, although touted as a prime concern in some sections of the globe, e.g., Europe, is not viewed as competitively important by North American manufacturers. Finally, volume flexibility is significantly less important today and in the future than product flexibility, e.g., high-performance, sophisticated, innovative products.*

STRATEGIC PRIORITIES BY INDUSTRY AND MARKET CLASSES

Further insight can be gained by a more detailed look at the differences in the responses according to different sales segmentation (mostly domestic, mixed, and mostly international) and industry classifications (manufacturing vs. nonmanufacturing). Figures 22 through 33 show the average responses grouped by international/domestic sales mix and manufacturing versus nonmanufacturing groupings. There are several interesting differences between the groupings, although some caution should be taken in interpreting the results because of the relatively small number of cases in some of the groups.

In Figure 22, we can see that product/service innovation as a future strategic priority is viewed as moderately important in competing successfully over the next five years for all groupings except nonmanufacturing firms operating mostly internationally.

Another interesting difference is the importance of competing on low prices for each of the subgroups (see Figure 23). While all groups ranked this as relatively unimportant compared to the other competitive strategies, the mostly international group had a mean rating of 4.22 compared to the mean for the mostly domestic group of approximately 5.0.

Interpretation: *This indicates that the business units that are competing internationally have realized the importance of competing on other factors besides price. In fact, the biggest differences overall in the different strategies is between the mostly domestic and the mostly international sales groups. Competitive pri-*

FIGURE 22
PRODUCT/SERVICE INNOVATION BY INTERNATIONAL/DOMESTIC SALES MIX

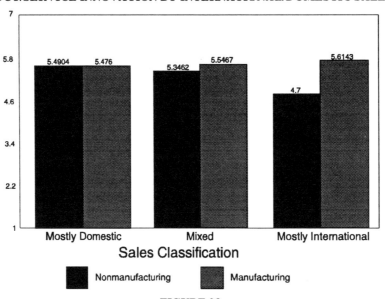

FIGURE 23
LOW PRICES BY INTERNATIONAL/DOMESTIC SALES MIX

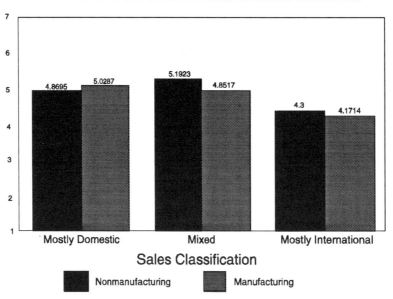

FIGURE 24
RAPID VOLUME CHANGES BY INTERNATIONAL/DOMESTIC SALES MIX

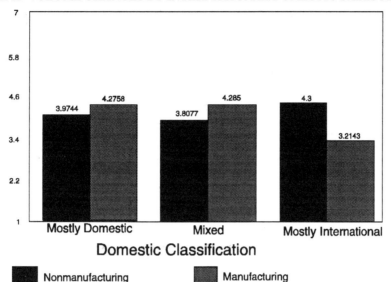

orities for international firms are different from domestic-oriented firms in competing successfully over the next five years. It is likely that procurement strategies will also differ to support domestic versus international sales.

At a time when the economy is overheating and capacity is constrained, rapid volume change might be an important competitive factor. Today the economy is more global and flexible and the ability to change volume rapidly is far less important. This reasoning is substantiated by the low rating given to this factor by all industry groups and sales classifications as demonstrated in Figure 24. Another interesting difference is in

the varying "lack of" importance of rapid volume changes. The international manufacturing group has the lowest mean rating of 3.2 while the international nonmanufacturing group has the highest average rating, 4.3. This is contrasted with the domestic and mixed groups where the manufacturing segments have a greater emphasis on rapid volume changes than the nonmanufacturing segment.

The mostly international nonmanufacturing group has the lowest average rating for the strategic importance of quality to future competitiveness (mean rating equals 5.5 out of a possible seven; see Figure 25).

FIGURE 25
HIGH QUALITY BY INTERNATIONAL/DOMESTIC SALES MIX

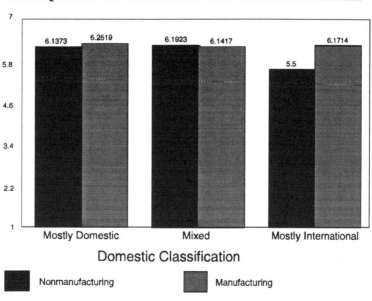

Interpretation: *The mostly international non-manufacturing group may have decided that high quality, although important, is no longer an order winning characteristic in the highly competitive international marketplace and may have realized that while high quality is certainly an order qualifier, other factors are more important in developing a competitive advantage. For all other groups, quality is the critical future competitive priority.*

Figure 26 documents the responses of the various groups on the strategic priority of providing high performance products and/or services. All groups view this factor as an important strategic priority. The only statis-

tically significant difference lies between the mostly international manufacturing and nonmanufacturing groups.

The hypothesis that quality is viewed as an order qualifier tends to be supported by the fact that this group has further differentiated itself in the mean relative importance of fast deliveries (mean rating equals 6.3 out of a possible seven; see Figure 27), dependable delivery (mean rating equals 6.3 out of a possible seven; see Figure 28), customer service (mean rating equals 6.5 out of a possible seven; see Figure 29), environmental concerns (mean rating equals 5.3 out of a possible seven;

FIGURE 26
HIGH PERFORMANCE BY INTERNATIONAL/DOMESTIC SALES MIX

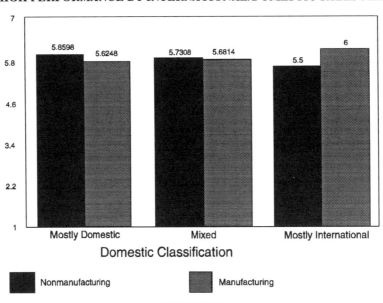

FIGURE 27
FAST DELIVERIES BY INTERNATIONAL/DOMESTIC SALES MIX

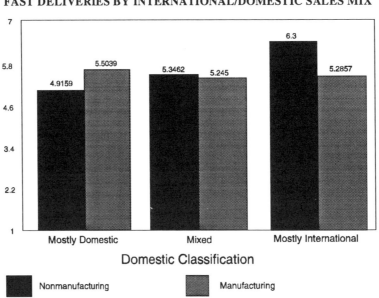

34

FIGURE 28
DEPENDABLE DELIVERY BY INTERNATIONAL/DOMESTIC SALES MIX

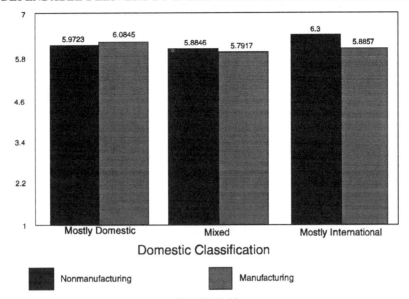

FIGURE 29
CUSTOMER SERVICE BY INTERNATIONAL/DOMESTIC SALES MIX

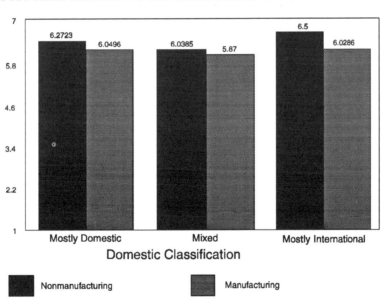

FIGURE 30
ENVIRONMENTAL CONCERNS BY INTERNATIONAL/DOMESTIC SALES MIX

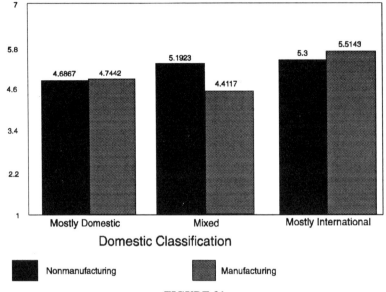

FIGURE 31
PROCESS INNOVATION BY INTERNATIONAL/DOMESTIC SALES MIX

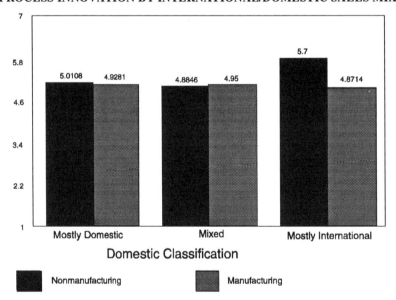

see Figure 30), and process innovation (mean rating equals 5.7 out of a possible seven; see Figure 31).

Interpretation: *In all of these categories, the mostly international nonmanufacturing group had the highest mean rating except in environmental concerns where it was slightly behind the international manufacturing group. On these six competitive priorities, domestic oriented and internationally oriented firms will likely develop different strategies for future operations.*

Figure 32 provides a summary analysis of strategic priority categorized by sales classification, Mostly Domestic, Mixed, and Mostly International. In this figure, the mean response for each group has been categorized into three different classes. Class 1, "**Primary Thrust,**" encompasses those strategic priorities, with an average rating score of 6.00 and above, with 7 being the maximum value. Class 2, "**Secondary Thrust,**" encompasses those strategic priorities, with an average rating score of 5.0 through 5.99. Class 3, "**Also Rans,**" encompasses those strategic priorities, with an average rating score equal to or less than 4.99.

FIGURE 32
STRATEGIC PRIORITY CATEGORIZATION BY SALES CLASSIFICATION

Strategic Priority	Mostly Domestic	Mixed	Mostly International
Product/Service Innovation	1	2	2
Low Prices	3	3	3
Rapid Volume Changes	3	3	3
High Quality	1	1	2
High Performance	2	2	2
Fast Delivery	2	2	2
Dependable Delivery	1	2	1
Customer Service	1	2	1
Technology Leadership	2	2	2
Customization	3	3	2
Environmental Concerns	3	3	2
Process Innovation	3	3	2

FIGURE 33
STRATEGIC PRIORITY RANK-ORDER BY INDUSTRY GROUP

Strategic Priority	Manufacturing	Nonmanufacturing
Product/Service Innovation	5	6
Low Prices	8	10
Rapid Volume Changes	12	12
High Quality	1	2
High Performance	4	4
Fast Delivery	6	8
Dependable Delivery	3	3
Customer Service	2	1
Technology Leadership	7	5
Customization	10	7
Environmental Concerns	11	11
Process Innovation	9	9

It is interesting to note that there is a clear difference in strategic emphasis, "Thrust," depending upon the sales orientation of the business unit. While firms with primarily domestic operations intend to emphasize innovation, quality, dependable delivery, and customer service, firms with mostly international operations intend to emphasize fewer priorities, namely, dependable delivery and customer service. The clear implication is that the domestic market is viewed by these business units as more demanding and the domestic customers as more discriminating than their international markets and customers. This supports the generally held belief that the North American marketplace, because of its openness to international trade, has become one of the most competitive in the world. Business units with mixed sales seem to be somewhat confused about their priorities, with only "high quality" as a primary thrust but six other strategic priorities as secondary thrusts.

Figure 33 provides a summary analysis of strategic priority categorized by industry group, either manufacturing or nonmanufacturing. In this figure, the priorities have been rank-ordered by mean rating for each group. The groups are quite similar, but differ in one important way. The top strategic priority for manufacturing firms is delivering a high quality product, while the top strategic priority for nonmanufacturing firms is delivering excellent customer service. This difference is not unexpected but does highlight the thought processes of the two industry groups.

The strategic priority with the greatest response class difference is "customization." The nonmanufacturing industry group views this strategic priority as significantly more important than the manufacturing industry group. This is quite different from the prevailing opinion offered in the popular press, which frequently touts the advantages of "mass customization."

THE STRATEGIC PRIORITY OF VARIOUS GROUPINGS OF RESPONDENTS

There are several other ways to analyze the differences in strategic emphasis. Those analyses as reported herein are by the business unit category of respondent (i.e., plant, division, group, or company); by the type of products/markets of that business unit (i.e., capital goods, consumer goods, industrial goods, consumer services, or industrial services); by the average reported return on sales (ROS) of the respondents; and by customer satisfaction performance. These analyses are provided in Figures 34 through 44. For succinctness, only the areas that have statistically significant differences will be specifically interpreted in this report even though many additional analyses were performed by the investigators.

Strategic Priority by Business Unit Category

The only significant difference with regards to the business unit is in the amount of emphasis placed on process innovation. In this case the division level placed a substantially lower level of emphasis on process innovation than did the company level. The division level is also less than the plant and group levels. The business unit may be less involved in the process changes than the plant level and may not be placing as much strategic importance on process innovation compared to the group and company level (see Figure 34).

Strategic Priority by Type of Products/Markets

Figures 35 through 37 show three areas that are substantially different according to the products/markets in which the business operates. Consumer goods-oriented firms place considerably more importance on rapid volume changes than any of the other groups and there is a statistically significant difference between the consumer goods market and the consumer services market (see Figure 35). The consumer goods' short product life cycle may be influencing the importance of this

FIGURE 34
PROCESS INNOVATION BY BUSINESS UNIT

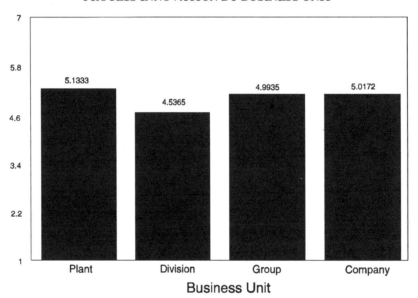

FIGURE 35
RAPID VOLUME CHANGES BY PRODUCTS/MARKETS

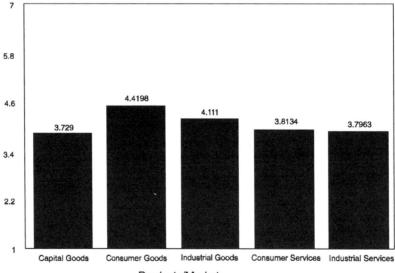

FIGURE 36
FAST DELIVERIES BY PRODUCTS/MARKETS

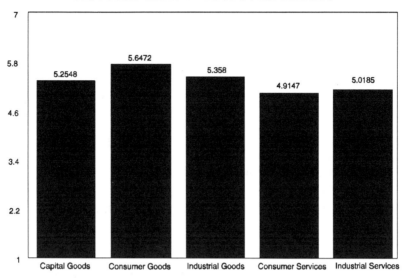

Products/Markets

FIGURE 37
CUSTOMER SERVICE BY PRODUCT/MARKETS

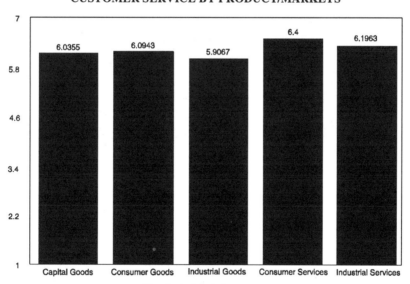

Products/Markets

strategy in that consumer goods are characterized by rapid innovation and product introduction.

A similar relationship can be found with regard to the importance of fast deliveries. The consumer goods market places significantly more emphasis on fast deliveries than the consumer services market (see Figure 36). This is logical since the giant consumer goods retailers, e.g., Wal-Mart, Kmart, and Target, are pressuring suppliers to help them increase inventory turns through fast and more frequent deliveries. Wal-Mart, for example, has a policy to penalize suppliers financially for any incomplete or late delivery.

Finally, Figure 37 shows that the industrial goods market places significantly less emphasis on customer service than do the consumer services market. Again, this finding is entirely logical.

Strategic Priority by Return on Sales

The relative importance of the different priorities can also be compared across the average return on sales (ROS) and the level of customer service. The respondents were clustered into three groups based on their performance on the Return on Sales (ROS) variable— Low, Average, and High return on sales.

Figure 38 shows that there is a significant difference in the emphasis placed on product/service innovation between group 1, the group with the lowest average ROS over the last three years, and group 2, the average group with respect to ROS. The low group places significantly less emphasis on innovation than the average group. This suggests that the degree of product/service innovation has a moderately important impact on profitability.

The low group on ROS also had significantly less emphasis on producing high performance products/services than the average ROS group (see Figure 39). The high ROS group placed even more emphasis on producing high performance products/services than did the low or average ROS groups, but because of the relatively small number of business units in that group, it did not come out as statistically significant. Clearly, the production of high performance products/services is highly correlated with an increasing average return on sales.

It is interesting to notice that the only statistically significant differences in the ROS clusters were due to product/service innovation, along with producing high performance products/services. One could hypothesize that these are two important areas of future competitive-

FIGURE 38
PRODUCT/SERVICE INNOVATION BY RETURN ON SALES

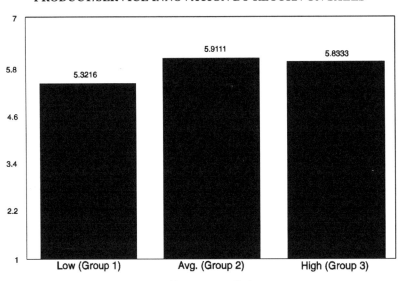

Return on Sales

FIGURE 39
HIGH PERFORMANCE PRODUCTS/SERVICES BY RETURN ON SALES

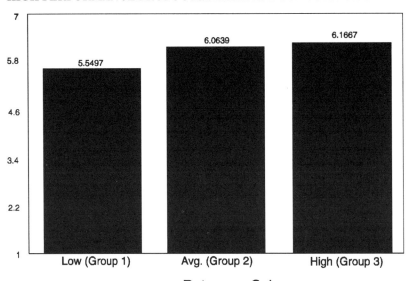

Return on Sales

ness in which poor performers, those with a low return on sales, are being left behind.

Strategic Priority by Customer Satisfaction Category

Figures 40 through 44 examine the statistically significant differences between the different future competitive priorities and the level of customer satisfaction provided by the respondents. Once again, the respondents were clustered into three groups based on their performance on the customer satisfaction variable— Low, Average, and High levels of customer satisfaction. The first significant difference is with the level of im-

portance of product and service innovation (Figure 40). The business unit group with the lowest level of customer satisfaction also placed the lowest emphasis on product/service innovation. This difference is statistically significant between the low cluster and the high cluster groups.

There is also a significant difference on the amount of emphasis that is placed on high performance products/services. In this case, group number three (the high group on customer satisfaction) is significantly higher then either the low or average group on customer satisfaction (see Figure 41). Firms that produce high performance products and/or services seem to stress

FIGURE 40
PRODUCT/SERVICE INNOVATION BY CUSTOMER SATISFACTION

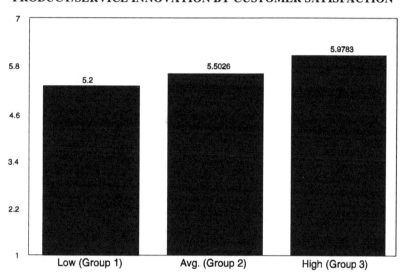

Customer Satisfaction

FIGURE 41
HIGH PERFORMANCE PRODUCT/SERVICES BY CUSTOMER SATISFACTION

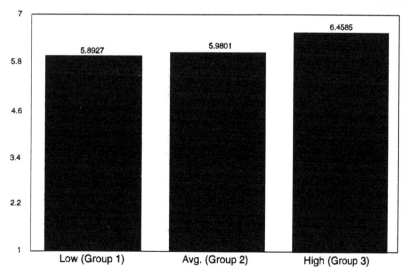

Customer Satisfaction

41

customer satisfaction. This is logical given the technical help *requirements* of the customers for these products and/or services.

A similar relationship exists with the degree of emphasis placed on dependable delivery and customer service. The high performers (group 3) have a significantly greater emphasis on both of these strategies than do either of the other two groups (see Figures 42 and 43).

The last strategy with a significant amount of difference for customer satisfaction is product/service customization. In this case, the group low on customer satisfaction (Group 1) has placed a significantly lower emphasis on product/service customization than the average (Group 2) and high (Group 3) groups (see Figure 44).

Interpretation: *Business units manufacturing innovative, high-performance products and/or services and emphasizing customer service through dependable delivery, and product and/or service customization have attained a high level of customer satisfaction.*

FIGURE 42
DEPENDABLE DELIVERY BY CUSTOMER SATISFACTION

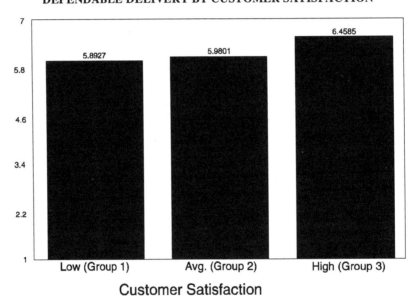

Customer Satisfaction

FIGURE 43
CUSTOMER SERVICE BY CUSTOMER SATISFACTION

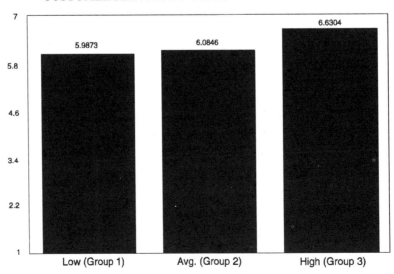

Customer Satisfaction

42

FIGURE 44
PRODUCT/SERVICE CUSTOMIZATION BY CUSTOMER SATISFACTION

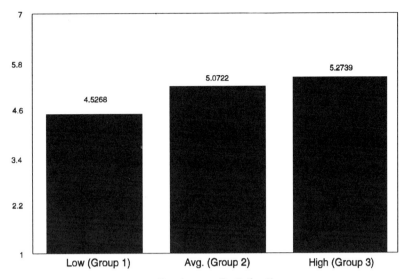

THE FUTURE EMPHASES OF PURCHASING AND SUPPLY MANAGEMENT

The rest of the questionnaire focuses on the degree of emphasis the business unit will place on various purchasing and supply management activities <u>over the next five years</u> (see question 12 in the questionnaire provided in Appendix A). The respondents rated 36 different activities stating whether they will place *increasing* or *decreasing emphasis* or *no change* in these activities over the next five years. For ease of analysis and interpretation, the responses were coded so that the number "1" represented the end point at *decreasing emphasis,* the number "4" corresponded to *no change* in emphasis, and the number "7" represented the end point at *increasing emphasis.* Figure 45 summarizes the responses to question 12.

From the figure, one can see that the five *most important* future activities in descending order are the use of Electronic Data Interchange (EDI) with suppliers (mean rating equals 5.68); supplier strategic alliances (mean rating equals 5.67); the increased use of information technology (mean rating equals 5.58); reducing purchasing transaction costs (mean rating equals 5.58); and purchasing systems and services (mean rating equals 5.55). The five *least important* future activities for respondents in increasing order of importance are third-party purchasing (mean rating equals 4.12); reverse logistics (mean rating equals 4.56); flattening the purchasing organization (mean rating equals 4.61); co-location of supplier and buyer firms (mean rating equals 4.62); and the use of supplier councils (mean rating equals 4.64).

Interpretation: *These results are rather surprising. Most of the bottom five activities are considered by some to be cutting-edge strategies. One possible hypothesis might be that firms interested in these topics have already implemented the activities, so less emphasis in the future is needed. There is some justification for this conclusion. In our case studies and conversations, many executives stated that purchasing and supply management organizations had already been significantly flattened and relatively less additional effort would be expended on this activity in the future. It is also possible that the practitioners see these activities as fads, and are not planning to spend much time or effort on them until they have a proven track record.*

This interpretation brings up an important consideration for the reader of this report. Simply because respondents fail to rate an activity as a high priority for future emphasis does not mean that they had not emphasized these activities in the past.

BUSINESS UNIT DIFFERENCES IN STRATEGIC EMPHASIS

The 36 activities were also analyzed by comparing the means according to business unit category (plant, division, group, and company), the products/markets categories (capital goods, consumer goods, industrial goods, consumer services, and industrial services), the domestic/international mix of sales, and the net profit before taxes as a percentage of sales. Only the topics where there was a statistically significant difference will be specifically presented in this report.

The future importance of purchasing and supply management performance measurement systems to the

FIGURE 45
FUTURE EMPHASES FOR PURCHASING

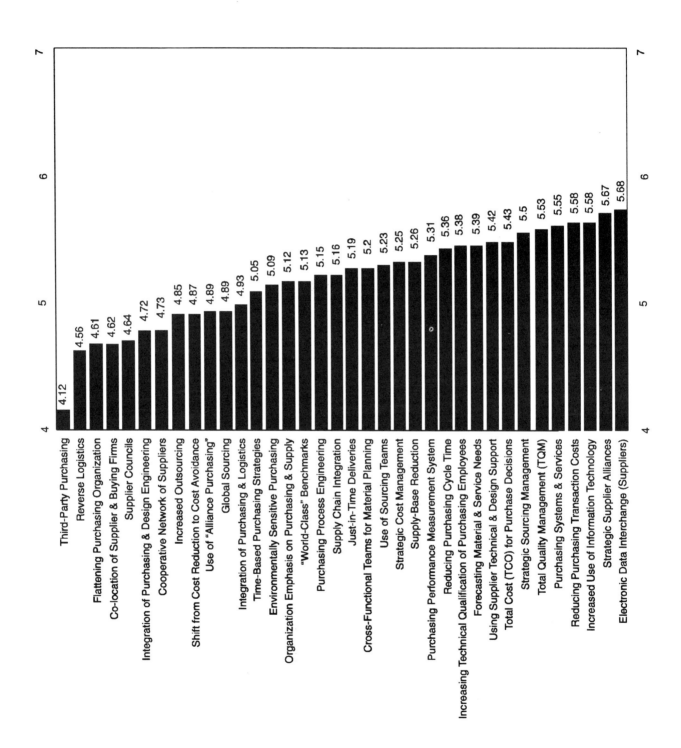

plants is significantly less than it is to the other groups. This may be a result of a greater reliance on centralized purchasing and supply management coordination (see Figure 46) by all groups. With less purchasing and supply management happening at the plant level, performance measurement systems should be less important at those plants.

The plant level is also less concerned with developing cooperative networks of suppliers than the other unit groups, although there is only a statistically significant difference when comparing at the company level (see Figure 47). This is entirely logical given that such supplier coordination requires a company-level effort.

Figure 48 shows the last significant difference at the business unit level. There is significantly less emphasis placed on purchasing and supply management process reengineering at the plant level, than at either the division or company levels. All of the aforementioned differences seem logical.

PRODUCT/MARKET DIFFERENCES

The industrial services and consumer services product groups are statistically different from both consumer goods and industrial goods product groups on the topic of global sourcing (see Figure 49). This difference is not surprising considering that the manufactured goods market, both industrial and consumer, has a higher need for materials, in general, than the service industry and services, in general, cannot be inventoried. Therefore, the manufactured goods manufacturers are more likely to search globally for the best source of supply.

The other area in the product market category that has a significant difference is in the strategic shift by purchasing and supply management from cost-reduction to cost-avoidance activity (see Figure 50). In this case, the industrial goods market is planning to place less emphasis on cost avoidance than the consumer services market is planning in the future. It seems that the industrial goods market is still caught up in cost reduction versus cost avoidance as a primary road to future competitiveness.

SALES MIX DIFFERENCES

There are three different activities that have statistically significant differences when compared on the domestic/international market mix. The first topic, strategic sourcing management, is not as important to the domestic sales group as it is to the mixed sales and mostly international sales groups (see Figure 51). Business units that are facing a more competitive environment in the international arena may have realized the importance of developing strategic sourcing plans and goals.

Global sourcing is also of greater importance to the mixed sales and mostly international sales groups than it is to the mostly domestic category (see Figure 52).

In both of these last two examples, the future activities being stressed by mostly international sales groups have *correlated strongly* with the mixed sales group. The reason that this difference is not statistically significant is because of the relatively small number of respondents in the mostly international group.

FIGURE 46
PURCHASING PERFORMANCE MEASUREMENT SYSTEM BY BUSINESS UNIT

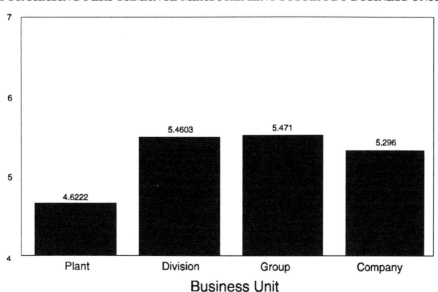

FIGURE 47
COOPERATIVE NETWORK OF SUPPLIERS BY BUSINESS UNIT

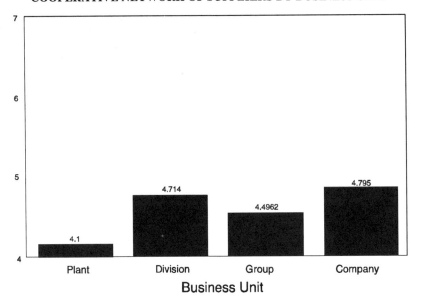

FIGURE 48
PURCHASING PROCESS REENGINEERING BY BUSINESS UNIT

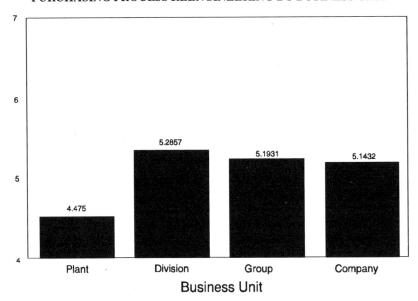

FIGURE 49
GLOBAL SOURCING BY PRODUCTS/MARKETS

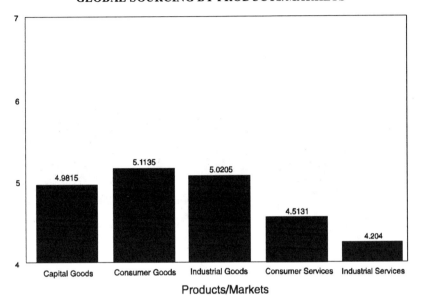

FIGURE 50
COST AVOIDANCE BY PRODUCTS/MARKETS

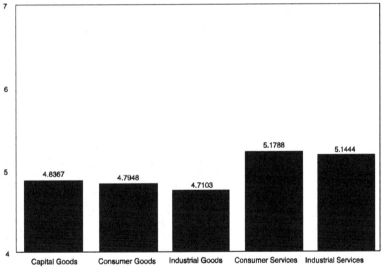

FIGURE 51
STRATEGIC SOURCING MANAGEMENT BY DOMESTIC CLASSIFICATION

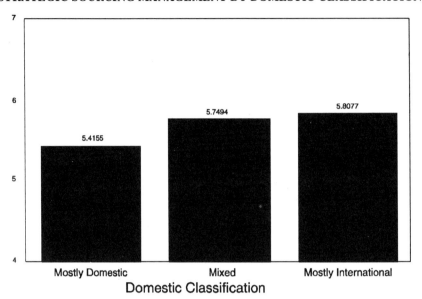

Domestic Classification

FIGURE 52
GLOBAL SOURCING BY DOMESTIC CLASSIFICATION

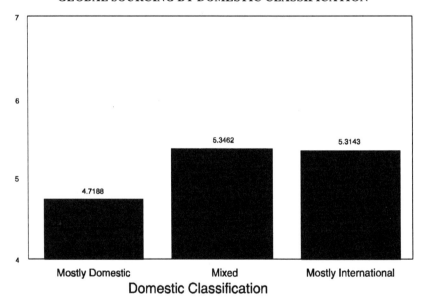

Domestic Classification

The third area of difference is cost avoidance. The mixed sales group is much less concerned with the future of this issue than are the mostly domestic sales and mostly international sales groups (see Figure 53).

DIFFERENCES IN NET PROFIT BEFORE TAXES

Figure 54 shows the only significant difference when the international/domestic sales groups are compared on net profit before taxes as a percentage of sales. The high net profit group places considerably more emphasis on the use of alliance (cooperative) purchas-

ing than do either the average net-profit or low net-profit groups.

Appendix E contains the statistical analyses performed on the collected data-base.

FIGURE 53
COST AVOIDANCE BY DOMESTIC CLASSIFICATION

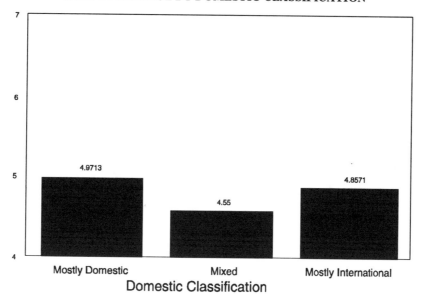

FIGURE 54
USE OF ALLIANCE PURCHASING BY NET PROFITABILITY

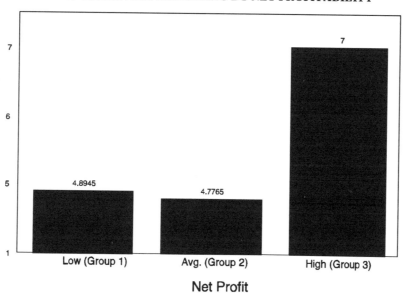

CORPORATE CASE STUDIES •

This chapter describes the case study data collected from the companies visited during the data collection phase of the project. The purpose of these visits was to gather qualitative data that would help identify emerging and anticipated future trends in purchasing management as seen by these companies that participated in the field study. The sizes of the firms, their products, and the industries they represent vary. The "case descriptions" do not follow a standard format. Instead, they are written so that essential information gathered during open-ended interviews are presented succinctly, leading to the identification of future and emerging trends.

The data collection was aided by an interview guide (containing open-ended questions) relating to purchasing futures. At the beginning of each visit, the authors explained to the respondents the purpose of the project and the nature of the information being sought. That is, the major trends that are in place in their industry and their firm, and how those trends in their view affected purchasing management activities.

It is to be noted that the firms the researchers visited are neither fully representative of any particular industry, nor do they constitute a random sample. The authors had to rely on voluntary participation from these companies and therefore these case descriptions represent a "convenience sample" of firms.

COMPANY A: PERSONNEL DEVELOPMENT FOR THE FUTURE

The main functions of Purchasing in Company A, a service organization, are planning and management of the company's purchasing strategy; preparation, negotiation and management of supply contracts; ongoing order processing and delivery of goods to the company's warehouses and end users; continuous quality improvement of all products and supplier processes, and resolution of quality issues and problems with suppliers. In Company A, purchasing practices and policies are called "acquisitions process." Purchasing spans the continuum from purchase order processing to strategic acquisitions. Because the firm is primarily a service provider, the links with sales and marketing are strong. Total value of purchases in Company A in 1993 was approximately $3.0 billion, encompassing a base of more than 5,000 qualified suppliers.

Purchasing is centrally managed but the organization fosters a decentralized task orientation. The strategic importance of purchasing has evolved over the years with increasing responsibility for quality, customer satisfaction, inventories of procured parts and distribution, and procurement engineering. Purchasing staff, many of whom have engineering training, work closely with Engineering in developing innovative solutions to customers problems and help engineering provide quick response to customers. Purchasing has adopted an "accounts management" perspective. Company A resorts to cross-functional teams and matrix management to focus the organization on customer satisfaction. Purchasing can "educate" its internal customers (through its membership on cross-functional teams) on the complexities of the procurement process and the value-added expertise that the purchasing staff brings to projects. Company A translates its customer strategy into a purchasing process strategy, which in turn is translated into an employee strategy which is used to define roles and responsibilities and to identify training needs. This mapping of corporate strategy into employee strategy is carried out under the rubric of TQM. Such a mapping allows employees to clearly align their efforts with customer-oriented strategies and priorities of the firm. Company A uses a process called "post delivery quality reporting" to handle customer problems. In tier 1, the customer will be helped by an engineer trained in quality-related problems. If a satisfactory resolution is not achieved, in tier 2, the problem will be handled by a quality analyst. If the problem is identified as relating to product design, in tier 3, it will be handled by specialists who can undertake a simulation of the products performance. Company A's goal is to provide a satisfactory solution to customer problems in two weeks. Since purchasing is partly responsible for quality assurance, the purchasing staff are involved in an important way in this customer-oriented effort.

Company A's mission statement for purchasing identifies market responsiveness, risk management, and lower life-cycle cost as the goals. Pursuant to these goals, Company A has developed an engineering economics-based decision-support system capable of addressing various cost components over a 5-to-7-year period in a discounted present value model, assessing the level of risk in large investments and performing statistical analysis of inventory, maintenance, procurement, and other costs.

Company A is pursuing supply chain integration as a strategy for reducing cost, increasing its responsiveness and providing "viable solutions" to its customers. Strategic sourcing is viewed as a necessity for accomplishing business objectives. The respondents from Company A identified the following as future trends in their firm:

- Purchasing's mission will be to help its customers achieve their business objectives, thus requiring greater degree of integration with other functions and a "market orientation";

- Purchasing will have a closer alignment with corporate strategy, not merely product and process strategies;

- Conventional purchasing will diminish. Maximization of profits and business growth will become more important than minimization of cost;

- Purchasing will become a critical asset to marketing; and

- Environmentally friendly business posture will influence purchasing strategies.

COMPANY B: FUTURE STRATEGIC ROLE OF PURCHASING

Company B is a manufacturer and distributor of a diverse set of consumer products. Company B has aggressively embraced the ideas of strategic sourcing and supply chain integration in managing its business. The discussion with the respondents focused primarily on the firm's efforts to operationalize these paradigms. Therefore, the main thrust of this case description is strategic sourcing and supply chain integration.

Company B has identified four key strategies for supply management. Company B is actively engaged in supplier consolidation as a strategic initiative. Starting at a supply base of 1,400, Company B has reduced the number of suppliers to 450. The ultimate goal is to continue with consolidation and further reduce the number of suppliers. The effort to rationalize the supply base is aided by "industry analysis," which encompasses the following aspects: industry outlook, supply and demand profile for the future, supplier pricing analysis based on a cost model (so that reliance on competitive bidding process can be reduced), emerging technological developments, and identification of the top quartile suppliers. Company B defines a continuum of suppliers who fall into one of four categories:

- Class I - "Arm's-length relationship"
- Class II - "Collaborative"

- Class III - " Partnership" and
- Class IV - " Strategic Supplier Partnership."

Company B has a systematized approach to evaluating suppliers for possible membership in Class III or Class IV. It begins with an assessment and internal analysis of a supplier's organization by a cross-functional team comprised of personnel from plant operations, research and development, the strategic business unit, and purchasing. The assessment of a suppliers operation includes the following dimensions: quality management systems, statistical process control, inventory management practices, process flow, reliability, and flexibility. The following three criteria relating to Company B's manufacturing plants are used in the evaluation of suppliers. These are called key performance indicators (KPI):

- downtime due to poor material or unavailability

- supplier "service" - quality of incoming material, on-time delivery, and accuracy

- supply inventory (days of on-hand inventory).

The third strategy used by Company B is "supplier synchronization," which relates to synchronous manufacturing. The supplier's production runs closely match the use of material in Company B's plants. The objective of such synchronization of production runs is to reduce inventory levels in the system. Inventory management responsibility is being passed on to suppliers through a pull system. Suppliers will have direct access to Company B's manufacturing database so that they can make appropriate production run decisions at their plants.

The fourth element of Company B's strategy pertains to "supplier improvements." Company B views dollar savings, quality, and service improvements as "enablers" for establishing a partnership relationship with a supplier. Strategic supplier partnerships (SSP) are viewed as "high-profile opportunities" with "strategic suppliers." Company B's executive team, along with executives from a supplier firm, initiates the process for strategic supplier partnering. At this stage a mission statement is developed for such a partnership and strategic objectives are defined. A partnering team, consisting of representatives from various functions in Company B and the supplier firm, develops action programs pursuant to the strategic objectives. Ad hoc teams in both organizations are then given the responsibility for the execution of action plans. The team's work on specific projects and are disbanded at the conclusion of the projects.

Several new initiatives are under way in Company B. Organizationally, buyers were in key industry categories. They have been moved to strategic supply management positions. This move is recognized by the company as warranting new skills in its purchasing staff : strong leadership and team-leading skills, ability to carry out supplier assessments leading to strategic supplier partnership, and project management skills. Recognizing the importance of these skills, Company B has established a "university" within the company to train strategic supply managers in project management, influence management, and leadership. The company has moved to a strong cross-functional orientation to set up a "seamless supply chain management" philosophy.

In the future, purchasing staff will be expected to satisfy more diverse expectations — that is, "buying things" to managing relationships with suppliers, leveraging suppliers' knowledge to introduce product innovations, and managing cycle times and quality. To do these effectively, purchasers must understand quality audits, financial stability of suppliers, and potential business risks to the company.

COMPANY C: HORIZONTAL NATURE OF PURCHASING'S FUTURE RESPONSIBILITIES

Company C is a multinational firm that manufactures complex, technology-intensive capital equipment. The assembly operations in its manufacturing facility are labor intensive. Although Company C is still a market leader, competitive pressures are growing. Company C is well known for its high-technology product. Its customers are demanding a high degree of customization, and the need to reduce cycle time is growing. Company C is pursuing the twin goals of a 25-percent reduction in cost and a 50-percent reduction in development time. To accomplish these twin goals while preserving its market leadership, Company C is aggressively restructuring its manufacturing, design, and purchasing functions.

The central aspect of this restructuring is the "responsibility-center" concept. The responsibility center is viewed as a "manufacturing business unit." The responsibility-center concept is much broader than the cost-center concept. The responsibility-center concept focuses the organization's efforts by gearing organizational structures, systems, and resources to satisfy customer demands and market needs. Company C refers to its approach as focused manufacturing, in which key processes are integrated to achieve corporate business goals. The links to the product and the market are stronger than what might be found in a traditional cost center (with an internal and operational focus). Company C uses "integrated build teams" to design and manufacture its products. The use of integrated build teams in responsibility centers stems from a company-wide strategy to transform itself into a high-performance organization.

The responsibility centers (columns) correspond to major subsystems that make up the product. There are as many responsibility centers as there are subsystems. The functions involved in designing and building the product — for example, tooling, design, and purchasing — constitute the rows, thus forming a matrix. The interfunctional build teams assigned to the responsibility centers have complete responsibility for their "product." In this process-integration model, purchasing staff are part of the integrated build team and take direction from the project (team) leader. Execution of purchasing's responsibilities is decentralized at the team level. Concurrent engineering is incorporated into each build team as part of the responsibility-center concept. Purchasing professionals have technical training so that they can be full-fledged members of the integrated build team. Company C identified the following benefits of employing the responsibility-center concept:

- reduced cycle times
- change in organizational culture
- expertise is where it needs to be
- flatter organization
- team development and cross-functional integration
- shorter communication channels, and
- empowerment of teams.

In Company C, traditionally, purchasing has not been viewed as a strategic strength. However, increasing demands from customers for higher levels of customization is causing Company C to resort to outsourcing as a strategy. Company C sees itself evolving into a "systems integrator," which would entail increasing the level of purchased components and subsystems. Company C will rely on suppliers for customization. As this happens, purchasing will gain in strategic importance. Company C respondents observed that purchasing will have increasing responsibility for "improving the product" and for helping the design teams in achieving "target costs." Recognizing the central role that cross-functional teams will play in responsibility centers, Company C is engaged in intensive training for its purchasing staff. Purchasing staff are expected to take the responsibility for "the product" instead of "the job."

Company C's global customers and worldwide markets, and the realities of international trade necessitate the purchase of major subsystems from international suppliers. Purchasing staff are involved in an important way in structuring these agreements with international suppliers. They are also involved in supply base management activities in which Company C has established local manufacturing operations pursuant to international trade agreements. These activities are expected to increase as Company C expands into rapidly industrializing markets in China and other Asian countries in the pan-Pacific region.

COMPANY D: PLANNING FOR PURCHASING CHANGE

On October 19, 1993, Company D was presented a prestigious honor as one of America's best-run plants. After spending time with Company D, it was obvious that both manufacturing management at Company D and the judging panel viewed the purchasing function and materials management as a critical factor in Company D's success. Purchasing at Company D is "no longer just a tactical subset of manufacturing" but a strategic part of Company D's supply management system. This case study documents why Company D was recognized as one of "America's Best Plants" and how the role of purchasing has changed and is changing at Company D.

Company D is a publicly owned company with approximately $6 billion in sales that provides products, systems, and services that increase comfort, environmental protection, energy conservation, productivity and safety in homes and buildings, aviation and space, and industrial process and manufacturing applications. Company D's business unit, with approximately $1.74 billion in sales designs, configures and assembles a family of systems that enables its customers to achieve world-class process control capability within their plants and products. Company D's customer base includes aircraft manufacturers, chemical process plants, oil refineries, food and consumer goods facilities, and pulp and paper mills around the globe. Company D views its particular missions as (1) providing customers with integrated plant solutions to improve productivity, yield, quality, and return on investment and (2) designing process control systems that help customers meet environmental and safety regulations. Given these missions, it is no surprise that at Company D no two customer "system solutions" are exactly the same.

In 1989, two facts gave Company D cause to reexamine its internal and external relationships. First, Company D's non-U.S. sales were growing faster than its U.S. business. It is estimated that by the end of the century, non-U.S. sales will approximate 50 percent of the total business. Second, a "paradigm shift around quality" was developing. The perception of quality was moving toward the idea of total customer satisfaction from one of defect prevention. These perceptions gave impetus to a multiyear world-class manufacturing effort that established progressive goals in three main areas: defect prevention, cycle-time reduction, and materials management optimization. Material represents nearly 70 percent of Company D's cost structure. Company D's executives knew that they needed to understand much more intimately the relationships and cost drivers within materials management in general and purchasing in particular. Company D decided that it must draw competitive advantage from the global integration of its marketing, purchasing, engineering, and manufacturing activities.

Within Company D, the purchasing function began to examine several critical issues.

- Can suppliers affect speed to market?
- Can suppliers influence cost and by that profit?
- Can suppliers provide technology critical to products, services, and customer solutions?
- Can suppliers influence Company D's ability to delight their customers?

The examination of these questions showed clearly that purchasing could become a strategic part of Company D business. Purchasing realized that it was in the business of "Supply Management" and not simply purchasing. The materials management function at Company D knew that it must develop a future-oriented program that would help it to better understand the business, think strategically, and build credibility with other functions. Some activities undertaken by Company D materials management to better understand their business processes are provided in Figure 55; other ventures allowed in order to think and act strategically are presented in Figure 56; and tasks performed to build

FIGURE 55
COMPANY D: ACTIVITIES UNDERTAKEN TO
UNDERSTAND ITS BUSINESS PROCESSES

FROM	TO
Knowing little about your company's products.	Attending company's sales/customer training.
Speculating about organizational roles.	Starting a week in the life of" rotation program.
Waiting to be invited to a critical planning meeting.	Get a sponsor and attend the meeting.
Routinely reviewing internal issues in department meetings.	Inviting guest speakers and reciprocating in their meetings.

FIGURE 56
COMPANY D: CHANGE IN THOUGHT AND BEHAVIOR

FROM

Allowing engineering to source components.
Managing by short-term budgets.
Thinking too small regarding hiring and talent.
Always following other companies' ideas.
Informally hearing about new products.
Being consumed with firefighting.
Thinking SMALL.

TO

Co-locating and joining engineering on new designs.
Developing a long-term strategy.
Developing and executing a long-term strategy.
Establishing high standards for people.
Participating on concurrent development teams.
Organizing to prevent fires.
Thinking BIG.

credibility throughout the organization are listed in Figure 57.

Building credibility within the organization allowed Company D materials management the means to undertake a progressive, future-oriented plan to improve materials management's strategic contribution. Some major accomplishments in materials management through 1993 have been:

- Organized by Supply Management, Acquisition Management, and Design Materials, realizing improved customer support and major productivity gains.

- Ninety-six percent of new product's components sourced with preferred suppliers.

- Materials management personnel are co-located in engineering, projects, and manufacturing.

- Reduction of active production supply base from more than 700 to fewer than 300 suppliers.

- Formation and management of 37 supplier quality "partners."

- Improved incoming quality from 5 percent defective to less than 0.5 percent.

In addition, the materials management function has developed a strong supplier strategic alliance program that has been developing "custom supply solutions" to help synchronize material flow from suppliers with manufacturing demand. A special team of materials management people created a matrix to classify purchase items according to the predictability of need and dollar amount expended. Using this matrix the team then develops a series of supply alternatives such as shared scheduling, use of resident suppliers, Just-in-Time, Electronic Data Interchange, and supplier stocking and kitting programs that are suitable for each commodity type and plant application.

What has materials management done for Company D lately? Materials management has implemented the "Aspect" component data base system to better plan new product solutions with customers. A new value engineering organization was formed composed of 12 engineers and materials personnel with $8 million in cost reductions to date. Materials management has finalized a documented Company D materials strategy that supports divisional marketing and manufacturing strategies and firmly cements the concept of materials management as a strategic weapon at Company D.

COMPANY E: PURCHASING ORGANIZATIONAL CHANGE FOR THE FUTURE

In the early 1980s, Company E realized the importance of supplier quality when it saw its market share in the semiconductor and communications sectors of the electronics industry begin to decline. Japanese competitors were successfully using JIT principles and supplier quality initiatives against U.S. electronics firms. Company E management studied the problem and familiarized themselves with the Japanese JIT philosophy and Japanese quality and defect standards. Out of this analysis came Company E's supplier-quality philosophy.

FIGURE 57
COMPANY D: BUILDING PURCHASING CREDIBILITY

FROM

50% of employees with college degrees.
Judging internal performance qualitatively.
Being passive about communications.
Being isolated from key customers.
Focusing on production procurement.
Lacking supplier performance data.
Comparing internal results to historical trends.

TO

82% of employees with college degrees, 25% with advanced and engineering degrees.
Demonstrating performance quantitatively.
Creating newsletters and project reviews.
Co-locating to creating cross-functional expertise.
Excellence in total business materials and services.
Creating a performance measurement system.
Actively benchmarking and looking outside-in.

Company E's supplier-quality development plan began in 1983 with the announcement of significant reductions of the supplier base. This reduction was the precursor to in-depth investments of time and resources with the remaining suppliers to significantly improve quality. In 1984, Company E centralized the Material Quality Engineering (MQE) function into one division and, simultaneously, began a formal supplier corrective action system. Realizing that a more concerted effort was needed in order to implement such an ambitious program, Company E later decided to manage the supplier base more closely through the formation of a Supplier Review Board (SRB). The SRB was the collection of the MQE, Reliability & Components Engineering, and Purchasing functions. The success of the SRB showed the need within Company E for a formal department that specialized in the management of supplier quality. In 1990, Company E combined the MQE, Reliability & Components Engineering, Purchasing, Incoming Inspection, Cost Analysis, and Proposal functions into what was termed the Supply Management organization (SM) structure.

At Company E, the manager of the SM organization reports directly to the office of the group General Manager (Executive Vice-President). This direct reporting relationship has allowed SM to inject many supplier-quality initiatives throughout the Company E group. In addition, it showed to each of the group's divisions the emphasis that Company E was placing on supplier quality management. Some initiatives pioneered by SM were early supplier involvement, standard parts, and SM input during product design. Before the development of the SM organization, Company E would rely upon its highly skilled design engineers and reliability and component engineers to pioneer new ideas. Suppliers would become involved in the process during the bidding stage of the procurement cycle.

Communication with their customers is very important at Company E. It has become a key initiative for Company E as a Total Customer Satisfaction program. The Total Customer Satisfaction program was begun to enhance communication with and responsiveness to customers and to provide products and services that completely satisfy the customer's needs.

Aggressive quality and customer satisfaction goals were set at the beginning of 1990. At this time, supplier quality was below 90-percent lot acceptance rate, 70-percent on-time delivery, and more than 3,000 suppliers were being used annually. Today, SM is experiencing a lot acceptance rate in excess of 98 percent, 90-percent on-time delivery, and an optimized supply base of approximately 800 vendors.

Other key targets for SM are the standardization of components, continuous improvement of supplier proc-

esses, and the establishment of "design-to" suppliers. Company E continues to strive toward total customer satisfaction as evidenced by aggressive key initiatives for 1993 and 1994. These initiatives include having all supplier processes under statistical control, eliminating all inspection of incoming material, and the use of EDI with all suppliers.

Incoming inspection is an integral part of SM. Before the formation of SM, an average lot would require more than a week to go through the inspection cycle. Today, the average lot takes less than a day for the same cycle and the goal is to eliminate inspection entirely. This will be accomplished through certified parts and certified supplier programs. Each program requires an "approved supplier" status and an excellent quality rating.

A continuous improvement perspective and philosophy is the key to SM's success. Company E has embraced the philosophy of continuous improvement throughout the company and is channelling this requirement through the supplier network. The goal is more than just "Zero Defects." The ultimate goal is to reduce variation and cycle time in every area. This philosophy has resulted in significantly improved quality, lower costs, reduced waste, shorter development and cycle times, and improved productivity. The inevitable goal is total customer satisfaction.

Supply Management Commodity Teams

The SM organization consists of seven commodity teams: passive, connectors, mechanical, microwave, semiconductor, active, and MRO (Maintenance, Repair, and Operating supplies). Commodity teams are responsible for the daily management of purchasing, quality, and reliability of the various families of components. Each team is responsible for supply base optimization, standard parts, certified parts program, failure analyses, pricing agreements, supplier corrective actions, and supplier quality surveys. The commodity teams' activities are divided among two area groups, purchasing and engineering. Both groups work toward common goals, but each has specific tasks.

The role of the purchasing group is to administer the buying of components and materials for Company E. Duties include placing orders, monitoring delivery schedules, supporting engineering requests, administering pricing agreements, communicating with suppliers, and generally supporting all program needs. The buyers themselves focus on long-term pricing agreements and supplier interfacing, and they are continually working toward reducing the purchasing system cycle time.

Engineering group activities can be separated into two categories: material quality and commodity engineering. A material quality engineer is responsible for supplier quality surveys, certified parts programs, dispositioning of defective material, and supplier corrective action. A commodity engineer is responsible for part-failure analysis, helping with design reviews, creating standard parts lists, supporting cost analyses and negotiations, and supplier problem solving. At Company E, these tasks are combined into several commodity teams and overlap in all of them. The main function of the engineering staff is to provide technical interfacing between the engineering function and suppliers.

Suppliers

Suppliers are evaluated and selected based on technology, quality, financial stability, management attitude, on-time delivery, on-site assessments, responsiveness, and price. No one category is considered significantly more important than the others, but price is considered the first among equals. Company E is a government contractor, and government contractors are required to justify their supplier selections based on cost effectiveness. To date, Company E has not been able to accurately place a figure on total quality and supplier attitude that would satisfy government requirements.

The continuous improvement philosophy is channelled down to suppliers. Each approved supplier must have a continuous improvement plan. Continuous improvement concepts that are expounded to suppliers are total quality management, process capability, SPC, implementation methods, individual responsibility, customer/supplier partnerships, and training.

Company E supports supplier efforts by helping key suppliers in the application of these concepts. Engineers visit suppliers to train, implement process control evaluations, and implement statistical process control (SPC). The commodity teams are responsible for enforcing and instituting continuous improvement plans at suppliers.

Since the formation of the SM organization structure, Company E has developed partnerships with many of its key suppliers. Business forecasts and long-term price agreements help suppliers in controlling inventory and establishing long-term agreements with *their* suppliers. In addition, suppliers have allowed Company E to examine their processes and exchange valuable manufacturing techniques. Improved supplier quality has been the result of these partnerships. When problems do arise, suppliers are willing to work with Company E to carry out fast, permanent, corrective actions.

Supplier Status

At Company E, suppliers are categorized into three classes: approved, restricted, and suspended. *Approved*

suppliers are targeted for long-term partnership and recommended for use in new designs. All standard parts must be obtained, whenever possible, from an approved supplier. Approved suppliers are sent a request-for-quote (RFQ) on all relevant orders. Classification as an approved supplier requires a minimum lot acceptance quality rating of 95 percent, and also a continuous plan for improvement. An acceptable continuous improvement plan includes process-control procedures and supporting controls on all critical and major parameters identified in applicable drawings, specifications, or purchase orders, a documented training program, management commitment, and a fast response to corrective action requests.

A supplier is classified as *restricted* if the supplier is deemed to have minimal future application within Company E but is necessary to support present programs. Restricted suppliers require management sign-off before the placement of a purchase order. Suppliers may also be placed on restriction for poor quality, nonresponsiveness, and substandard delivery performance. Restricted suppliers are required to have a Risk Planning Assessment visit if orders are more than $2,500, lead times are longer than two months, the supplier is on the U.S. mainland, and the quality rating is below 95 percent.

Suppliers are classified as *suspended* when no future business is anticipated. The suspended list prohibits programs from buying materials from these suppliers. Very poor suppliers are usually found on this list.

Certified Supplier Programs

A key aspect of Company E's supplier quality initiative is the implementation of a dock-to-stock flow of materials. Dock-to-stock means that materials flow directly from a supplier's shipping dock to Company E's production line without incoming inspection or receiving at the company dock. To ensure adequate and economical control of material, supplier-responsible defective part information is collected and analyzed to evaluate supplier conformance. Company E has accomplished dock-to-stock flow of material by instituting programs that certify specific parts and part types of selected *approved* suppliers. Entire operations and facilities have been certified.

Company E initially began its certified parts program in 1990 with the creation of the Approved Manufacturers Parts Program (AMPP). AMPP was initiated and controlled by the SM function. The Supplier Review Board (SRB) reviews and selects candidates for the program. To be considered for AMPP, a supplier must have an approved status, a 100-percent lot-quality history on the last 13 lots received for standard parts or 33 lots received for nonstandard parts, a 100-percent acceptance rating on the last 500 parts inspected, and statistical process control (SPC) procedures carried out on all critical and major characteristics. SPC data are reviewed quarterly at Company E, and meetings are held with the supplier at least once a year. An on-site quality survey is required once every two years to verify the process control program and continuous program plan objectives.

Another dock-to-stock program is the Distributor Inspection Certification Program (DICP). As the name implies, the program is targeted toward distributors and not original manufacturers. The objective of DICP is to eliminate inspection at Company E and do it at the distributor's facility. DICP candidates must have an approved status, 100-percent acceptance quality rating for the last three months, and the ability to perform inspection at their facility. Other criteria are similar to the AMPP, except that restricted suppliers and nonapproved suppliers' parts may be used on DICP.

The benefit for suppliers being on either AMPP or DICP is that SM must RFQ them on all orders that relate to their line of business. AMPP suppliers are also designated as "design-to" suppliers and must be considered first for all new design introductions.

SUMMARY OF CASE STUDIES

This chapter has described the case study information obtained through discussions with representatives from participating companies. Company A case data suggests these main trends: a higher degree of technical training for purchasing personnel, a closer link with markets and customers, a strategic orientation toward supply management activities, an expansion of purchasing responsibility to include quality engineering, quality assurance, and customer satisfaction, and an emphasis on total cost of purchases, decision models and supply base rationalization.

Company B case data suggest the following trends: increasing strategic role of purchasing, increasing need for training in leadership and influence skills, integration of information systems with suppliers, development of tools and techniques for partnering with suppliers, and broadening influence of sourcing decisions across the value chain.

Company C case data suggest that purchasing personnel in the future will work "outside" the purchasing department as part of integrated, cross-functional teams, their share of the responsibility for products and customer satisfaction will grow and that as market demands for customization and flexibility increase, the role and importance of purchasing will change.

Have these changes stated in the Company D case study had an effect on Company D's performance? Absolutely. Company D has experienced some spectacular gains. For example, from 1990 to 1993 internal defect rates have been reduced by 70 percent in the ISO 9000-certified facility. Customer rejects are down 57 percent. Lead times for parts shipments to customers were cut by 72 percent. Using the "custom supply solutions" concept mentioned earlier, investment in materials for major product lines has been reduced by 46 percent. Warranty costs have been reduced by 30 percent. Manufacturing cycle time has been compressed by 89 percent. Work-in-Process inventory as a percentage of revenue has decreased 89 percent. Finally, manufacturing costs were reduced by 30 percent over this same period.

Supply Management (SM) organizational structure has had a major impact on the way Company E does business. With the major emphasis leaning towards controlling supplier quality and managing the supply base, Supply Management will play an even greater role at Company E in the future. The large increases in quality, on-time delivery, and customer satisfaction experienced by Company E have been important for product competitiveness. Improving the last one or two percent in each category to a truly zero-defects condition is the challenge that lies ahead for Supply Management.

When viewed collectively the case studies suggest that the observed trends can be grouped into organizational/structural changes, changes in "skill mix," changes in scope of responsibilities, and change to a market orientation. These ideas are incorporated into the discussion in the final chapter that deals with the results of the study.

SUMMARY AND IMPLICATIONS •

The framework used in this manuscript encompassed four distinct sections: (1) the Executive Purchasing Roundtables in North America and Europe, (2) the survey data analysis and development of a descriptive model, (3) the corporate case study exploratory analysis, and (4) the Purchasing Futures Symposium at Michigan State University. Each of these sections yielded unique insights into purchasing and supply management's changing future role in the corporation.

THE EXECUTIVE PURCHASING ROUNDTABLES

There were many areas of difference between the North American and European Roundtable participants. Some of these differences can be explained by culture, a short-term versus longer-term planning orientation, and varying focuses on cost reduction through better information management and effectiveness measures.

It seemed apparent to the investigators that cultural differences was only one factor impacting the difference in future directions reported for both executive purchasing and supply management roundtables. A more significant factor was the size of the firm and rate of evolution of purchasing and supply management. For example, larger firms saw a greater need to increase the technical ability of purchasing and supply management employees than smaller firms. Also, it was apparent to the investigators that the rate of evolution within the purchasing and supply management and supply management arena was more pronounced in North American industries. Part of this difference can be attributed to the need for European firms to plan for the integration of a common market within the continent. For example, the use of sourcing teams by European firms was predicted to increase dramatically as Europe moves to a common supply and logistics marketplace.

There was a clear sense expressed in North America that better information systems and technology was the route being taken to cost reduction and, ultimately, cost avoidance. The Europeans felt that this demonstrated North America's orientation to short-term planning and gains while they, the Europeans, were more longer-term oriented by stressing effectiveness measures rather than efficiency goals. For example, a European manager stated that "Europe has gotten the message that we are in a long, hard fight, but North America has not gotten the message yet." The investigators do not entirely agree with this statement but report it here as a basis for understanding the perceptions of each group of managers.

THE DESCRIPTIVE MODEL

The primary objective of this section of the analysis was to further examine the data with the intent of uncovering any underlying concepts or key issues, called constructs, that impacted the respondents view of purchasing and supply management's future role in corporations. This task was accomplished using a relatively sophisticated social science tool called "Factor Analysis." The following eight key purchasing and supply management issues (factors) that *might have* an impact on purchasing and supply management's future role in corporations were uncovered.

- **Factor 1 - Supply Chain Management**

Key components of this factor were

1. Supply base reduction

2. The use of sourcing teams

3. Co-location of buyer and supplier

4. Purchasing and supply management process reengineering

5. The use of "World-Class" benchmarks

6. The implementation of supplier strategic alliances and

7. An emphasis by purchasing on implementing alliance purchasing agreements.

- **Factor 2 - Total Quality Purchasing Management**

Key components of this factor were

1. The use of total quality management (TQM) principles within purchasing

2. Increasing the technical qualifications of purchasing and supply management employees

3. Forecasting both material and service needs

4. A focus by purchasing and supply management on internal systems and services and

5. An increasing emphasis on purchasing and supply management performance measurement systems.

- **Factor 3 - Time-Based Purchasing**

Key components of this factor were

1. Use of time-based purchasing strategies

2. Strategic cost management

3. Just-in-Time deliveries

4. An organizational emphasis on purchasing and supply management

5. The use of cross-functional teams and

6. Using supplier technical and design support.

- **Factor 4 - Transaction Cost Management**

Key components of this factor were

1. The use of electronic data interchange (EDI) with suppliers

2. An emphasis on reducing purchasing transaction costs and

3. A thrust to reduce purchasing and supply management cycle time.

- **Factor 5 - External Organization Integration**

Key components of this factor were

1. The use of supplier councils

2. The development of a cooperative network of suppliers

3. Increased global sourcing activity

4. Supply chain integration and

5. Strategic sourcing management.

- **Factor 6 - Internal Organizational Integration**

Key components of this factor were

1. The strategic integration of the purchasing and logistics functions

2. The strategic integration of the purchasing and design engineering functions and

3. An increased use of information technology by purchasing.

- **Factor 7 - "Green" Purchasing**

Key components of this factor were

1. Environmentally sensitive purchasing and

2. Reverse logistics.

- **Factor 8 - Outsourcing**

Key components of this factor were

1. An increased use of third-party purchasing

2. An increased outsourcing of material and service needs and

3. A flattening of the purchasing organization.

Prior to developing a "bi-variate correlation-based" descriptive model that relates these eight purchasing and supply management futures factors to the various strategic competitive priorities stressed by the survey respondent firms, such measures of competitive strategic priority were calculated from the survey data. Toward this goal, 12 competitive priorities were factor analyzed in order to reduce them to a logical set of strategic composite factors to be used in the descriptive bi-variate correlation section of the analysis. One can interpret these four factors as *strategic themes* stressed by the respondents to the survey instrument:

- **Strategy 1 - Total Quality Focus**
- **Strategy 2 - Differentiation/Customization Focus**
- **Strategy 3 - The Traditional Purchasing Focus**
- **Strategy 4 - The Eco-Organization Focus**

Bivariate correlations coefficients were calculated using the eight previously defined future directions factors and the four previously defined strategic competitive priority factors. These correlations provided the following insights.

CORPORATE CASE STUDIES

The corporate case studies suggested several major trends: higher degree of technical training for purchasing and supply management personnel; closer link with markets and customers; strategic orientation and supply management activities instead of the traditional role; expanded responsibility of purchasing department to include quality engineering and assurance, and customer satisfaction; emphasis on total cost of purchases, decision models, and supply-base rationalization; increasing strategic role of purchasing and supply management; increasing need for training in leadership and influence skills; integration of information systems with suppliers; development of tools and techniques for partnering with suppliers; and broadening influence of sourcing decisions across the value chain.

In addition, corporate case study data suggest that purchasing and supply management personnel in the future will work "outside" the purchasing department as part of integrated, cross-functional teams. Their share of the responsibility for products and customer satisfaction will grow and that as market demands for customization and flexibility increase, the role and importance of purchasing and supply management will change.

Have these changes had an effect on performance? Absolutely. Company D experienced some spectacular gains. For example, from 1990 to 1993 internal defect rates have been reduced by 70 percent and customer rejects are down 57 percent. Lead times for parts shipments to customers was cut by 72 percent. Investment in materials for major product lines has been reduced by 46 percent. Warranty costs have been reduced by 30 percent. Manufacturing cycle time has been compressed by 89 percent. Work-in-process inventory as a percentage of revenue has decreased 89 percent. Finally manufacturing costs were reduced by 30 percent over this same period.

When viewed collectively, the case studies suggest that the observed trends can be grouped into organizational/structural changes, changes in "skill mix," changes in scope of responsibilities, and change to a market orientation. These ideas are incorporated into the development of 11 management propositions presented at the end of this chapter.

THE PURCHASING FUTURES SYMPOSIUM

Strategic planning, customer orientation, early supplier involvement, partnership, and Just-in-Time systems dominate the recent literature of purchasing and supply management. These ideas draw purchasers toward a view of their work that is far different from the traditional heavy paperwork, reactive buying actions, and price-oriented competition for which the buying community is known. All of these concepts are derived from technology and information systems that enable purchasers to visualize and measure the effect of their decisions in a manner not feasible even one decade ago. The cumulative effect of these approaches to purchasing and supply management is overall improvement in product quality, reduced cost of operations, and increased competitiveness throughout the economy.

The service perspective of purchasing and supply management has been useful in the past but no longer serves organizational goals well. Purchasing and supply management will have to become a regular player on the team, rather than a provider of towels, uniforms, and drinks. Key suppliers will also have to join the team. And the growing reliance on suppliers to provide goods and services formerly sourced internally is placing new demands on effective supply management. The purchasing manager *must* become a manager of external operations.

Many industrial trends and many more not covered in this manuscript (e.g., 24-hour production, global manufacturing, and rapid product realization) reflect this endless quest for a finish line that does not exist for purchasing and supply management. Only continuous improvement is considered a sustainable philosophy today. These trends are dominated by technological innovation and rationalization through integration and simplification throughout the supply chain. The details seem less important, but the reality of these trends is already upon us.

GUIDELINES FOR IMPLEMENTATION

First, the purchasing function in firms whose competitive direction is based upon a total quality priority should focus on developing the activities of electronic data interchange (EDI) with suppliers, an emphasis on reducing purchasing and supply management transaction costs, a thrust to reduce purchasing and supply management cycle time, the use of total quality management (TQM) principles within purchasing and supply management, increasing the technical qualifications of purchasing and supply management employees, forecasting both material and service needs, a focus by purchasing and supply management on internal systems and services, and an increasing emphasis on purchasing and supply management performance measurement systems.

Second, the purchasing function at firms whose competitive direction is based upon a differentiation/customization competitive priority should focus on developing the use of total quality management (TQM) principles within purchasing and supply management, increasing the technical qualifications of purchasing and supply management employees, forecasting both material and service needs, a focus by purchasing and supply management on internal systems and services, an increasing emphasis on purchasing and supply management performance measurement systems, strategic cost management, Just-in-Time deliveries, an organizational emphasis on purchasing and supply management, the use of cross-functional teams, using supplier technical and design support, the strategic integration of the purchasing and logistics functions, the strategic integration of the purchasing and design engineering functions, an increased use of information technology by purchasing, environmentally sensitive purchasing, and reverse logistics, that is, the role of logistics in recycling, reuse, waste disposal, and management of hazardous materials, and the movement of used materials "backward" up the supply chain from the customer to suppliers.

Third, the purchasing function at firms whose competitive directions are based upon a traditional competitive priority should focus on developing strategic cost management models, Just-in-Time deliveries, an organizational emphasis on purchasing and supply management, the use of cross-functional teams, using supplier technical and design support, the use of supplier councils, the development of a cooperative network of suppliers, increased global sourcing activity, supply chain integration, strategic sourcing management strategies, environmentally sensitive purchasing, and reverse logistics, that is, the role of logistics in recycling, reuse, waste disposal, and management of hazardous materials and the movement of used materials "backward" up the supply chain from the customer to suppliers.

Fourth, the purchasing and supply management function at firms whose competitive directions are based upon an eco-organization competitive priority should focus on supply base reduction, the use of sourcing teams, co-location of buyer and supplier, purchasing process reengineering, the use of "World-Class" benchmarks, the implementation of supplier strategic alliances, an emphasis by purchasing on implementing alliance purchasing agreements, the use of electronic data interchange (EDI) with suppliers, an emphasis on reducing purchasing transaction costs, a thrust to reduce purchasing cycle time, environmentally sensitive purchasing, and reverse logistics, that is, the role of logistics in recycling, reuse, waste disposal and management of hazardous materials, and the movement of used materials "backward" up the supply chain from the customer to suppliers.

ELEVEN MANAGEMENT PROPOSITIONS FOR THE FUTURE OF PURCHASING AND SUPPLY MANAGEMENT

This chapter discussed the results of the multiphase research study. The trends relating to purchasing and supply management futures identified by the researchers by employing a multifaceted approach to data collection are integrated into 11 propositions. These propositions are going to be important to the purchasing and supply management profession and are likely to shape the role that purchasing and supply management will play in attaining organizational goals. The implications of these propositions to purchasing and supply management practice is identified in which such unambiguous identification is possible. The investigators have refrained from drawing inferences where such inferences will be purely conjectural. The discussion of

the implications of these propositions dealing with purchasing and supply management trends does not include prescriptions as to how purchasing and supply management should react to these trends. Appropriate responses to these trends, to a great extent, will depend on organizational and contextual considerations that were not explicitly addressed in this research. It should also be emphasized that the main objective of data analysis in this study was not to develop prescriptive strategies for coping with current or emerging trends, but to identify such trends and to understand their implications.

Remember that the data collection was accomplished in three parts: first, the Purchasing Futures Symposium (focus group discussion) was used to identify the major trends in purchasing and supply management and in the related disciplines of logistics, manufacturing, new product development, government and international manufacturing; second, a large sample survey data were collected, and finally, the researchers conducted open-ended discussions with executives in five different firms, which were presented in the form of case studies. This "triangulated" approach to data collection yielded a rich base of information, albeit qualitative, from which to identify important trends.

Since the results of each source of data and their analysis or implications have been discussed in earlier chapters, we proceed directly to a discussion of the propositions, the supporting rationale, and their implications.

Proposition 1 : The strategic importance of purchasing and supply management will increase in the future. Purchasing and supply management will emerge as a key element of business strategy.

Purchasing and supply management has been viewed variously in organizations. Some organizations have viewed purchasing and supply management as infrastructural while others have viewed purchasing and supply management as part of the value chain relating to *material flow*. This narrow perspective is gradually being superseded by the realization that purchasing and supply management affects much more than the material flow along the value chain. This trend in organizations is being aided by several related trends in operations:

- Push for greater flexibility in manufacturing systems

- Technological intensity of products

- Need for high degree of customization

- Focus on customer preferences

- Globalization of markets

- "Lean manufacturing" practices and

- The need for "quick response" and time-based competition.

Most of these trends have cast the role and importance of purchasing and supply management in sharper focus than ever. Increasingly, in an effort to attain a high degree of manufacturing flexibility without prohibitively expensive capital investments, firms are beginning to rely on suppliers with proven manufacturing and technological capabilities. Customization demands and the need for "quick response" in rapidly changing market and business environments are also causing firms to realize the strategic role that suppliers and supply management can play in achieving sustainable, competitive advantage.

The spread of lean manufacturing concepts will further strengthen this strategic purchasing and supply management trend in the future. Lean manufacturing practices implies that purchasing and supply management will span a broader range of activities than traditional buying-related activities to include supplier qualification, certification, development, strategic alliances, management of JIT deliveries and, closer coordination of inventories and material flows. The emergence of this trend is also corroborated by the results of the survey, which identified supplier alliances, supplier development, and strategic sourcing management among the most prevalent trends. However, the case-study data suggest that purchasing and supply management executives will have a key role to play in "educating" other functions in the organization as to the strategic importance of purchasing and supply management. It appears that increasingly firms are relying on cross-functional training and job rotation to accomplish this.

Proposition 2: The strategic "reach" of purchasing and supply management will increase in the future.

Although lean manufacturing has brought to light the importance of sourcing and supply management, the primary view of purchasing and supply management in many organizations is that it interacts primarily with manufacturing and the suppliers. Strategic view of purchasing and supply management, however, demands that it be linked to the market and the customer, leading to the extension of the "reach" of purchasing and supply management all the way from suppliers through the internal value chain of the firm, to the market, and on through to the customer. This contention is underscored by the results of exploratory factor analysis of the survey data, which identified "internal integration" and "external integration" as two of the factors extracted.

In addition to the traditional cost focus, purchasing and supply management will increasingly stress "product focus" through such initiatives as concurrent engineering and quality assurance; "process focus" through interorganizational integration necessitated by elec-tronic interchange of product and manufacturing process data; "market focus" through benchmarking and helping the marketing of a firm's products through TQM and customer satisfaction initiatives; and "customer focus" through quality function deployment. The breadth of these activities suggests that the strategic reach of purchasing and supply management will increase in the future.

Support for this proposition was found in the survey data, the Purchasing Futures Symposium, and the field studies. The survey data identified TQM and customer satisfaction, total cost decisions, and forecasting needs of the firm as significant trends. Field-study data indicated that under emerging paradigms of organizational restructuring and management, purchasing and supply management will bear a greater share of *direct responsibility* for customer satisfaction than it has in the past.

Proposition 3: Purchasing and supply management will become management of external operations.

In organizations of the future, world-class operations will require world-class supply management and suppliers. Developing sustainable competitive advantage depends on developing competencies that are not easily duplicated by competitors. Supply management in world-class organizations will evolve into such a competency. As Leenders and Nollet, and David Burt have argued, purchasing and supply management will deviate from its traditional role as gatekeeper for all communications with suppliers. Interfaces to customers and suppliers will become more porous in the future, thus facilitating direct communication between suppliers and other functions within the organization. That is, business functions will be able to communicate directly with their counterparts in supplier organizations without having to go through purchasing and supply management.

As firms outsource more, the need for communication, coordination, control, and planning of interactions between the supply base and the firm increases. The survey data show that external and internal integration trends will continue or become stronger in the future. Due to these reasons, a greater share of what used to be done internally will have to be done outside the organization.

Management of external organizations will imply greater reliance on information technology, compatibility of planning and information systems, greater need for strategic sourcing and supply management. Purchasing and supply management professionals will require greater "general management" (i.e., interdisciplinary) training than they have had in the past. These assertions are also supported by the case studies.

Proposition 4: Strategic alliances with suppliers will increase in number and degree.

There is an apparent paradigm shift taking place in U.S. firms — a shift away from arm's-length relationships with suppliers to closer, carefully targeted strategic relationships with suppliers. This paradigm shift is necessitated by the new realities of competition and markets. The most significant focus in organizations these days is "time-based competition." In the future, organizations will have to manage time the same way that they have managed cost, quality, and delivery. Several components of time management can be identified: time to market (from concept to customer), ramp-up time for full-scale production, lead time for procured parts and systems, set-up time, distribution time, and response time for special requests and contingencies. Stalk in his *Harvard Business Review* article identifies *time* as the next source of competitive advantage. Suppliers will play a key role in time-based competition. These ideas are supported by the results of the survey data in that electronic data interchange (EDI), information technology, and reducing purchasing and supply management cycle time were identified as being among the most significant trends.

Lean manufacturing and synchronous manufacturing trends will continue to emphasize just-in-time production and delivery of components and subsystems. The degree of synchronization called for by these developments requires greater cooperation between suppliers and buying firms than has existed in the past. The degree of interorganizational integration will increase. These developments will drive the need for establishing "co-makership" or strategic partnerships with key suppliers.

Suppliers will continue to affect other competitive dimensions such as cost, quality, deliveries, service, and innovation of a company. As the push to integrate the supply chain into the business functions of a firm continues, and as markets and customers are more fully integrated with the operations of a firm, key suppliers and business firms will share a "co-destiny" as never before. These developments point to a shift away from a power relationship over suppliers to a partnership relationship with suppliers.

Concurrently with these developments, purchasing and supply management is receiving attention as a strategic strength of a firm. The strategic view of purchasing and supply management embraces such ideas as "capability buying," in which supplier competencies in design, development, and process technology are relied on for time compression and innovation; sharing of cost information; technical cooperation; and continuous quality improvements.

The trend toward strategic alliances with suppliers is supported by results of the survey data, in which it was identified as one of the most significant trends. This trend was also supported by the case studies. There are important implications stemming from this trend. First, organizations have to develop a systematic way for identifying partnership opportunities with suppliers. Such assessment must go beyond the traditional dimensions of cost, quality, and delivery. Firms must develop the capability to assess the *strategic fit* of a supplier's capabilities with the competitive (strategic) priorities of the firm. Partnerships with key suppliers should enable firms to satisfy current priorities as well as market opportunities in the future. Second, business growth and management of business risk will be shared by purchasing and supply management in the future. Partnership agreements and assessments need to reflect these. Purchasing and supply management will have to learn how to develop these partnership agreements into a strategic strength. This would entail appropriate target setting for supplier performance and competitive benchmarking.

Proposition 5: Purchasing and supply management will play a key role in strategic cost management in firms.

Although competition in the future will be based on time, innovation, customization, and technological capabilities, cost and quality leadership will continue to influence the ability of a firm to compete successfully. As firms shift their focus away from standard costing practices with their emphasis on allocation of overhead costs and rely more heavily on activity based costing and strategic cost management paradigms, purchasing and supply management's influence will grow. This contention is supported by several well-entrenched trends in accounting practices today.

The trend toward increased outsourcing reinforces the role of purchasing and supply management in strategic cost management. A greater share of a product's cost will be incurred "outside" the firm, thus necessitating careful consideration of costs of acquisitions. Life-cycle costing (which folds in the cost of owning the firm's product for a customer) and designing to a target cost both signal the increasingly important role that purchasing and supply management will play in strategic cost management in the future.

These contentions are supported by the results of the survey data. Reducing transaction costs and total cost decisions were identified as significant trends. In addition, transaction-cost management emerged as one of the factors in the exploratory factor analysis of the data. Support for this emerging role of purchasing and supply management was also found in the case studies conducted by the researchers.

63

Proposition 6: Verticalization of purchasing and supply management practices in organizations will increase.

This trend is suggested by the case study data and contemporary thinking in structuring organizations. Organizations are structuring themselves along "key business processes" that extend from suppliers across functional boundaries into a firm's customer base. This view of a business enterprise "stacks" the value chains or supply chains leading to the vertical distribution of functional specialists among the value chains. This view of the organization is in conformity with the flattening of organizational structures in general and with the concept of interdisciplinary teams in particular.

If this trend continues, purchasing and supply management expertise will reside in each of the distinct value chains leading to a "fragmentation" of purchasing and supply management skills and expertise. Purchasing and supply management staff will interact with the members of the cross-functional team — drawn from design, engineering, manufacturing, logistics, marketing, customer service/support, and packaging. Such a cross-functional team will have complete responsibility for concept to market of products, and other business objectives such as growth, profitability, market share, and customer satisfaction. Working in this environment would require different patterns of interaction and subscribing to different norms of behavior than what purchasing and supply management staff may be used to in the relative homogeneity of other purchasing and supply management personnel within a functional unit.

To function effectively, purchasing and supply management goals will have to be more closely aligned with the strategic goals of the firm relative to specific value chains. The training for the staff will have to emphasize teaming and project management skills. Purchasing and supply management personnel will be called upon to operate successfully, under potentially different priorities as they move from one supply chain to another supply chain. This implies that purchasing and supply management staff will be more business-strategy-oriented than purchasing and supply management-oriented.

The survey data support some of these inferences from qualitative case data in that technical qualifications of purchasing and supply management personnel, and forecasting of customer needs were among the most significant trends identified.

Proposition 7: Flattening of purchasing and supply management organizations will continue due to the use of horizontal, self-managed teams.

This trend is related to the verticalization of supply chains. Since purchasing and supply management activities will be distributed over a number of self-managed teams, the need for an extensive purchasing and supply management hierarchy will be less in the future. Purchasing and supply management personnel will receive direction from project directors and team leaders in the organization of tomorrow. Purchasing and supply management expert knowledge will be provided by central purchasing. Central purchasing will assume the role of knowledge creation and dissemination, especially on purchasing and supply management strategies and on how they relate to the strategic priorities of the firm.

Information dissemination within self-managed teams will be faster (since communication across different levels of hierarchy is obviated). Purchasing and supply management will be expected to respond more quickly to demands of the market and customer than under the traditional functional structure. Communication across supply chains will rely more on networking and teleconferencing than face-to-face communication.

Proposition 8: Management of the "white space" will become increasingly important for purchasing and supply management executives.

In the emerging view of organizations, functional hierarchies will be fewer. Horizontal corporations, with self-managed teams-in-parallel, will require less coordination and control of personnel within the purchasing and supply management organization. Instead, focus will shift to managing the interfaces that purchasing and supply management has with other functional units in each of the supply chains, thus leading to the expression "management of the white space." Purchasing executives will become more strategically focused. Their responsibility will shift to managing the strategic connections that purchasing has with other functions. Purchasing will have shared responsibility with project managers and team leaders for key business processes and their strategic contributions to the success of the firm.

Proposition 9: Purchasing and supply management will increasingly come under the influence of the new paradigm — "the learning organization."

Under emerging views of organization, the concept of the "learning organization" has received a lot of attention. Organizations will restructure and reengineer themselves to promote learning and acquire intellectual capital. In such organizations, employees are not only expected to continually improve their skill levels but to share their knowledge with others to create the learning organization.

As this paradigm gains acceptance, education and training for purchasing and supply management personnel will become broader (technical and managerial skills will be equally emphasized) to facilitate cross-functional team interactions more effectively. Areas of anticipated training will include routine use of corporate-wide, "electronic idea board," project management, leadership and influencing skills, and strategic cost analysis and modeling. Information dissemination among purchasing and supply management personnel will be faster through more intensive use of information technology (personnel computers, networking etc.). Just-in-time learning (related to the emerging idea of KANBRAIN philosophy) will dominate through the use of performance enhancement systems, tele-learning, and knowledge-exchange programs. Learning and job performance will be concurrent.

Support for these trends is provided by the results of survey data that identified the increasing use of information technology and the reengineering of purchasing and supply management processes and systems as significant trends.

Proposition 10: New realities of purchasing and supply management performance evaluation will emerge.

Purchasing and supply management performance evaluation will be more closely linked to business objectives — business growth, profitability, market share, customer satisfaction — in the future. The impetus for this trend stems from the "horizontal corporation," and the verticalization of supply chains. As key suppliers are integrated into the supply chain, and as purchasing and supply management is more closely linked to markets and customers, the ensuing strategic role of purchasing and supply management will dictate that performance evaluations be more closely linked to business goals of the firm.

Purchasing and supply management performance will be more closely linked to "external objectives" and "corporate-wide objectives." TQM and business process reengineering have focused the attention of firms on avoiding waste and non-value-added activities. In the future, focus in organizations will shift to "value creation" and "value maximization," as more firms adopt the concepts of "economic value added (EVA)" and "market value added (MVA)." Purchasing and supply management performance will be judged on the basis of the value it creates and the contribution it makes to value maximization. These trends also call for purchasing and supply management to be more strategically oriented than it has been in the past.

Proposition 11: Purchasing and supply management will emerge as a core competence of firms.

As the role of purchasing and supply management shifts from a "service provider" to a more strategic role, purchasing and supply management will be recognized as a core competence of a firm. Firms will be able to distinguish themselves from their competition through their purchasing and supply management competencies. Purchasing and supply management in the future will seek to develop competencies that are not easily duplicated. The implication of this for competitive benchmarking of purchasing and supply management practices is unclear.

POSSIBLE LOCUS OF EVOLUTION

The framework shown in Figure 58 is an attempt to link the various propositions relating to strategic purchasing and supply management, and supply management futures to specific trends and the competitive focus of the firm. The figure hypothesizes a possible locus of evolution both for competitive priorities and the strategic sourcing trends. In developing this model, the investigators are implicitly asserting that it is the evolution in the competitive focus that drives purchasing and supply management trends.

A quality/customer satisfaction focus will be associated with total quality purchasing and supply management management (TCPM) and total cost management (TCM). In the next stage of evolution, time-based competition and responsiveness will dominate the competitive posture of the firm. This will be associated with time-based purchasing and supply management strategies. In the next stage, competition will be primarily based upon differentiation, which will be associated with supply chain integration, strategic cost management, and increased outsourcing. Finally, firms that have achieved high levels of quality and customer satisfaction, time-based competition, and customer market responsiveness and product differentiation, will develop an "eco-focus" to further differentiate themselves from their competition. This last stage would be associated with "green" purchasing and supply management and reverse logistics. All 11 of the propositions relate to these associations.

MANAGEMENT IMPLICATIONS

These propositions have broad implications for purchasing and supply management in the future. The implications stemming from each of the propositions have been discussed above. The implications are grouped into "future purchasing and supply management organization," "future purchasing and supply management practices," and "future purchasing and supply management

FIGURE 58
STRATEGIC EVOLUTION OF PURCHASING FUTURES

STRATEGIC EVOLUTION OF PURCHASING FUTURES

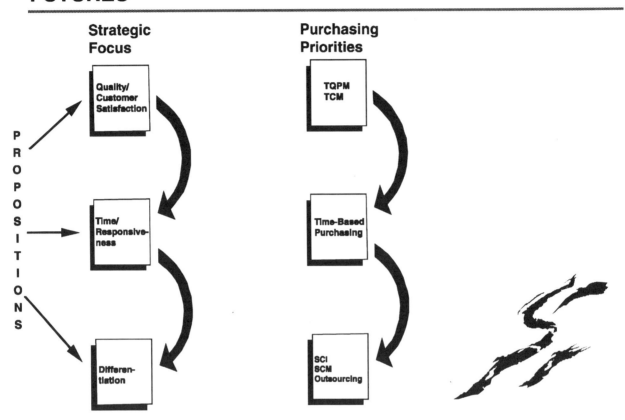

education and training" and presented succinctly in Figure 58.

Future Purchasing and Supply Management Organization

- Flatter purchasing and supply management organization
- Fragmentation (distribution) of functional expertise
- Verticalization of supply chains
- Membership in separate supply chains or key business processes
- Cross-functional team or project orientation

Future Purchasing and Supply Management Practices

- New realities of performance evaluation
- Teams in parallel
- Strategic focus

- Supplier alliances
- Supply chain integration
- Greater reliance on information technology
- Market/customer focus
- Total-cost decisions
- Strategic-cost management
- Greater internal integration across value chain
- Emphasis on time-based strategies
- Reduction of transaction-cost management
- Value maximization

Future Purchasing and Supply Management Education and Training

- Broader training to facilitate cross-functional team interaction
- Tele-learning and knowledge exchange
- Performance enhancement systems
- Concurrent learning and job performance

APPENDIX A: QUESTIONNAIRE •

PURCHASING FUTURES RESEARCH PROJECT

1. Principal product(s) manufactured by the business unit
    (specify SIC code if known):
    _____

2. Check the response that best describes the <u>business unit</u>:
    Plant [ ]   Division [ ]   Group [ ]   Company [ ]

3. Which category <u>best</u> describes the products/markets of the business unit?
    (<u>Check only one.</u>)
    Capital Goods[ ]   Consumer Goods[ ]   Industrial Goods[ ]
        Consumer Services[ ]   Industrial Services [ ]

4. What were the sales in dollars of the business unit in the last fiscal year?
    $ _____

5. What was the overall net profit <u>before tax as a percent of sales</u> for the
    business unit in the last fiscal year?
    _____ %

6. What was the approximate average annual growth rate of sales over the last
    three years for the business unit?
    _____%

7. What percentage of sales for the business unit are to domestic customers?
    _____%

8. What was the approximate average <u>Return on Sales</u> for the business unit over
    the last three years.
    _____%

9. Please indicate your business unit's overall rating on customer satisfaction
    compared to your competitors.(Place a check mark on the scale.)

    |_____ _____ _____ _____ _____ _____|
    1   2   3   4   5   6   7
    Poor   Average   Outstanding

10. How do you expect the mix of international vs.domestic sales for the business
    unit to change over the next five years? (Place a check mark on the scale.)

    |_____ _____ _____ _____ _____ _____|
    3   2   1   0   1   2   3
    Increased   No   Increased
    International   Change   Domestic

67

11. Place an X to indicate the **degree of importance** of each of the factors listed to the business unit in competing successfully over the next 5 years.

		Little or No Importance						Critical Importance
a.	Product/Service Innovation	1	2	3	4	5	6	7
b.	Low Prices	1	2	3	4	5	6	7
c.	Rapid Volume Changes	1	2	3	4	5	6	7
d.	Consistently High Quality	1	2	3	4	5	6	7
e.	High Performance Products/Services	1	2	3	4	5	6	7
f.	Fast Deliveries	1	2	3	4	5	6	7
g.	Dependable Delivery	1	2	3	4	5	6	7
h.	Customer Service	1	2	3	4	5	6	7
i.	Technology Leadership	1	2	3	4	5	6	7
j.	Product/Service Customization	1	2	3	4	5	6	7
k.	Environmental Concerns	1	2	3	4	5	6	7
l.	Process Innovation	1	2	3	4	5	6	7

THE FUTURE

12. Place an **X** to indicate the **degree of emphasis** the business unit will place on the following activities over the next 5 years. (If your org. is not using an activity now and does not plan to use the activity in the future, leave response blank.)

		Decreasing Emphasis			No Change			Increasing Emphasis
		-3	-2	-1	0	1	2	3
a.	Use of sourcing teams							
b.	Co-location of supplier and buying firms							
c.	Supply-base reduction							
d.	Increasing tech. qualif. of purch. employees							
e.	Total Quality Management (TQM)							
f.	Strategic sourcing management							
g.	Purchasing systems & services							
h.	Forecasting material and service needs							
i.	Using supplier technical and design support							
j.	Reducing purchasing transaction costs							
k.	Electronic data interchange (suppliers)							
l.	Strategic supplier alliances							
m.	Supply chain integration							
n.	Increased outsourcing							
o.	Flattening the purchasing organization							
p.	Cross-functional teams for material planning							
q.	Purchasing performance measurement systems							
r.	Just-in-time deliveries							
s.	Environmentally sensitive purchasing							

		Decreasing Emphasis		No Change		Increasing Emphasis

t. Total Cost (TCO) for purchase decisions

| -3 | -2 | -1 | 0 | 1 | 2 | 3 |

u. Supplier councils

| -3 | -2 | -1 | 0 | 1 | 2 | 3 |

v. Cooperative network of suppliers

| -3 | -2 | -1 | 0 | 1 | 2 | 3 |

w. Global sourcing

| -3 | -2 | -1 | 0 | 1 | 2 | 3 |

x. Time-based purchasing strategies

| -3 | -2 | -1 | 0 | 1 | 2 | 3 |

y. Strategic cost management

| -3 | -2 | -1 | 0 | 1 | 2 | 3 |

z. Org. emphasis on purchasing & supply

| -3 | -2 | -1 | 0 | 1 | 2 | 3 |

α. Shift from cost reduction to avoidance

| -3 | -2 | -1 | 0 | 1 | 2 | 3 |

β. Purchasing process reengineering

| -3 | -2 | -1 | 0 | 1 | 2 | 3 |

χ. Integration of purchasing and design engineering

| -3 | -2 | -1 | 0 | 1 | 2 | 3 |

δ. Integration of purchasing and logistics

| -3 | -2 | -1 | 0 | 1 | 2 | 3 |

ε. Increased use of info. technology

| -3 | -2 | -1 | 0 | 1 | 2 | 3 |

φ. Third-party purchasing

| -3 | -2 | -1 | 0 | 1 | 2 | 3 |

γ. Reducing purchasing cycle time

| -3 | -2 | -1 | 0 | 1 | 2 | 3 |

η. Use of "alliance purchasing"

| -3 | -2 | -1 | 0 | 1 | 2 | 3 |

ι. "World-Class" benchmarks

| -3 | -2 | -1 | 0 | 1 | 2 | 3 |

φ. Reverse logistics

| -3 | -2 | -1 | 0 | 1 | 2 | 3 |

APPENDIX B: GLOSSARY OF TERMS •

The following annotations contain explanations for some of the terms used in the questionnaire:

Alliance Purchasing: Firms teaming up to buy items from common suppliers. The motivation is to reduce costs, leverage buying operations, and foster economies of scale.

Co-location: The trend (or requirement in some cases) toward suppliers locating themselves close to the buying firm. This trend is very much in evidence with certain Japanese manufacturers. Increased emphasis on time-based competitive strategies (e.g., JIT Purchasing) might give impetus to co-location. There are also instances in which the supplier uses part of the manufacturing firm's facility for warehousing and staging operations.

Cooperative network of suppliers: This concept parallels the idea of Japanese Keiretsu. As firms enter into strategic alliances with first-level suppliers, the tendency might filter into second- and third-tier suppliers. Loose partnerships might be formed setting up a network of suppliers that dedicate themselves to helping the principal buyer achieve his or her competitive mission.

Cost Avoidance: This alludes to a proactive stance in getting the product to the market at the lowest price (or target price). Purchasing's analytical abilities are used "upfront" in the planning phase to squeeze cost out of the product (versus engaging in cost-reduction activities after the product hits the market).

Green Purchasing: This concept is an outgrowth of environmentally sensitive manufacturing (a strategic priority for Japanese, European, and many U.S. manufacturers). The degree to which environmental concerns dominate sourcing and supply management (including the purchase of products and services and source selections).

Reverse Logistics: The role of logistics in recycling, reuse, waste disposal, and management of hazardous materials. The movement of used materials "backward" up the supply chain from the customer to suppliers.

Sourcing Teams: Firms are increasingly using (cross-functional) teams to source and manage their supply base. Typical membership on the team includes purchasing, manufacturing, accounting, and customer service. The Commodity Action Team (CATs) concept used by several purchasing organizations is an example.

Strategic Alliance: The supplier is relied on for much more than simply a product or service. Supplier design skills and unique capabilities are primary considerations. Some of the design work and customization might be handled by the supplier. Supplier shares some of the risk and the rewards that accrue from long-term contracts and preferred supplier relationships. Supplier assumes the responsibility for meeting broad customer requirements.

Strategic Sourcing: This concept views sourcing as a strategic weapon. Supply management considerations stem from the competitive strategies of the firm. Sourcing is viewed as competitive strength and is involved in strategic planning. Sourcing strategies are explicitly identified and evaluated by top management.

Supply Chain Management: Managing the flow of materials and products through the value chain, from suppliers to ultimate customers. Requires integration across purchasing, operations, distribution and transportation.

Supply Chain Integration: Suppliers are an integral part of the business system of the buying firm. Information exchange is frequent or real-time using EDI. Suppliers are an important part of product/service development, design changes, etc. Suppliers have access to marketing plans, etc.

Supplier Councils: These are teams of suppliers that serve in an advisory capacity to the buying firm, helping to improve key business and manufacturing processes. The buying firm benefits through lower costs and improved processes; suppliers benefit by strengthening relationships and long-term contracts.

Third-Party Purchasing: Contracting out some of the buying activities. The main motivation is to reduce purchasing transaction costs by way of a leaner organization.

Time-Based Purchasing: Purchasing strategies that emphasize and enhance time-based competition. JIT purchasing, concurrent engineering, EDI, cycle-time reduction, and reengineering are examples.

APPENDIX C: COVER LETTER •

May 1994

Dear purchasing professional:

On September 1, 1993, a new research project began that could significantly impact the field of purchasing and materials management over the next decade and beyond. This project is called "**The Purchasing Futures Research Project**" and is sponsored by the Center for Advanced Purchasing Studies (CAPS). The project's goal is to develop a vision for what the purchasing function will look like as we move into the next century....roles, responsibilities, capabilities, organization, etc.

Phase I of the project entailed performing a computer-assisted, interactive assessment of what 68 participants at the CAPS Executive Purchasing Roundtable, all leaders in the purchasing and materials management field, felt were the critical issues impacting this function during the next five years and the implications of these issues.

As a result of executive discussions and company visits, the research team has generated the questionnaire enclosed with this letter. It has been sent to a diverse number of purchasing professional in various industries across the country. The questionnaire is thorough and your responses are **very important** to us. Please take a few minutes and complete the instrument. We guarantee that your individual responses will be kept **strictly confidential.**

Please mail your responses back to us as soon as possible in the enclosed envelope. Without your help, the most important segment of the project cannot succeed.

We want to share the results of this project with you. Simply send us one of your business cards along with the completed questionnaire in the enclosed return envelope. When the project is completed, we will send you a copy of the final report.

Thank you very much for your help in this project.

Sincerely yours,

Joseph R. Carter, D.B.A., C.P.M.
Associate Professor of Purchasing
Arizona State University

Ram Narasimhan, Ph.D.
Professor of Operations Management
Michigan State University

APPENDIX D: PURCHASING FUTURES SYMPOSIUM •

This appendix presents the papers delivered at the Academic Symposium on Purchasing and Materials Management Futures that was held at Michigan State University on December 4, 1993. The purpose of the conference was to bring together prominent researchers in the areas of purchasing and materials management, and the related areas of service operations, manufacturing, technology and product development, logistics, and international manufacturing operations.

The research methodology that was adopted for the study called for bringing together theoretical perspectives, information from a large sample survey data, and data from case studies. It was felt by the researchers that such a multifaceted approach was necessary to fully understand the purchasing trends that are in place and those that are in the offing. The Purchasing Futures Symposium, in particular, served two major purposes. First, it helped to explore one of the main objectives of the research, that is, understanding the implications of major trends that are developing in areas closely related to purchasing and materials management. Such understanding is necessary because of the important interfaces that exist between purchasing and the other functional areas within an organization. The motivation for this perspective stems from Porters, now widely accepted, value chain paradigm. Second, the ideas expressed in the presentations at the Purchasing Futures Symposium provided a basis for developing the survey instrument that was used in the subsequent large sample survey of industries.

As will be discussed in later chapters, many of the ideas that were expressed by the presenters at the Purchasing Futures Symposium pertaining to future trends were corroborated by the survey data, while some were disaffirmed. In a study that deals with future trends, it is difficult to rely only on quantitative analysis of survey data. A clearer picture is more likely to emerge if multiple sources of data and information are jointly considered and evaluated in identifying future trends. Such a procedure is also likely to lead to a clearer understanding of why these trends are in place and what guidelines can be given to exploit these trends to advantage.

The presenters in the Purchasing Futures Symposium were:

- John E. Ettlie, University of Michigan

- Harold E. Fearon, Center for Advanced Purchasing Studies

- Chan K. Hahn, Bowling Green State University

- Thomas Hendrick, Arizona State University

- Michiel Leenders, University of Western Ontario

- Jeffrey G. Miller, Boston University

- Stanley N. Sherman, The George Washington University

- D. Clay Whybark, University of North Carolina

The panel of presenters included NAPM Professors as well as prominent researchers who attempted to link research in their own areas to potential trends in purchasing. In what follows, the researchers have included the papers and presentations that were made at the conference. It is noted that these presentations are part of the "data" collected by the researchers in the course of the project.

NEW PRODUCT-PROCESS DEVELOPMENT TRENDS & LINKAGES

John E. Ettlie, Ph.D.
University of Michigan

Abstract

In 1975, Jim Utterback and Bill Abernathy published the final version of a paper detailing a dynamic model of product and process innovation. What have we learned about the product-process innovation process since then? What are the implications for materials and supplier management? Where do we go from here? These questions are addressed in this paper.

In particular, there appears to be at least five emergent trends in managing the productive segment of the firm that have implications for materials and supply chain management:

1. Systemic thinking: In particular, the **convergence of the technology and quality (including the ecofactory) agenda** of the business unit.

2. Joint production (i.e., flexibility and economies of scope) are likely to be enhanced by **co-production:** the actual sharing of productive facilities between suppliers and users.

3. The merging or conscious **reconciliation of supplier policies** for technology and component or service purchase. This includes a much more sophisticated approach to dealing with Universities.

4. The integration of purchase and engineering design data base management systems as part of greater emphasis on articulating and implementing **manufacturing strategies.**

5. The simplification and continued **integration and consolidation of supply chain** management through reduction of the number of first-tier suppliers and using such methods as JIT II and other mechanisms (e.g., AlliedSignal's order-to-remittance reengineering project) that promote an adaptive organization.

New Product-Process Development Trends & Linkages

One of the most influential models of the technological innovation process appeared in a series of articles starting with the precursor publication of Abernathy and Wayne[1] on the limits of the learning curve, and then on to the model itself which incorporated this learning curve principle in Abernathy and Townsend,[2] Utterback and Abernathy,[3] and Abernathy.[4] The model details the dynamic relationship between product and process innovation over the life cycle of a firm, a product and/or an industry. The purpose of this discussion is to review this model, evaluate where the field has been since its introduction and then engage in some informed speculation about where the field is headed, with special attention to material and supplier management.

For simplicity, the version of this model that appeared in Utterback and Abernathy[5] will be the focus of the discussion. To get things started, the term "productive segment" that was used as the core unit of analysis in earlier treatments was changed to the "production process," and was defined as "the system of process equipment, work force, task specifications, material inputs, work and information flows, etc., that are employed to produce a product or service."[6]

The overall model, which is summarized in Figure 59, predicts that the firm's strategy for competition and growth is specifically related, in one of three evolutionary stages, to the firm's propensity to host product or process innovations. In stage one, firms attempt to maximize product performance, and use unstandardized or general purpose equipment.

As companies move into stage two, they maximize sales by adopting more integrated automation — emphasizing process innovation over product innovation. When firms enter stage three, they have begun to become less innovative overall, while concentrating on cost minimization.

FIGURE 59
LEVEL AND TYPE OF INNOVATION

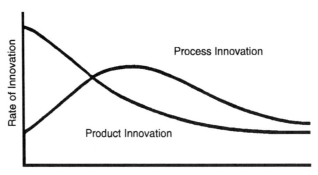

Time or product maturity

	Fluid Pattern	Transitional Pattern	Specific pattern
Competitive emphasis on	Functional product performance	Product variation	Cost reduction
Innovation stimulated by	Information on users' needs and users' technical inputs	Opportunities created by expanding internal technical capability	Pressure to reduce cost and improve quality
Predominant type of innovation	Frequent major changes in products	Major process changes required by rising volume	Incremental for product and process, with cumulative inprovement in productivity and quality
Product line	Diverse, often including custom designs	Includes at least one product design stable enough to have significant production volume	Mostly undifferentiated standard products
Production processes	Flexible and inefficient; major changes easily accommodated	Becoming more rigid, with changes occurring in major steps	Efficient, capital-intensive, and rigid; cost of change is high
Equipment	General purpose, requiring highly skilled labor	Some subprocesses automated, creating "islands of automation"	Special purpose, mostly automatic, with labor tasks mainly monitoring and control
Materials	Inputs are limited to generally available materials	Specialized materials may be demanded from some suppliers	Specialized materials will be demanded; if they are not available, vertical integration will be extensive
Plant	Small-scale, located near user or source of technology	General purpose with specialized sections	Large-scale, highly specific to particular products
Organizational control	Informal and entrepreneurial	Through liaison relationships, project, and task groups	Though emphasis on structure, goals, and rules

Source: From Abernathy and Utterback, "Patterns of Industrial Innovation," p. 40.

Punctuated Equilibrium

Other than the secondary data analysis results that Utterback and Abernathy[7] themselves report, little of any subsequent empirical testing has examined this theory directly.[8] The most identifiable intellectual legacy of the model, however, reemerges in Tushman and Anderson's work.[9] This punctuated equilibrium model of the innovation process is supported by data from the computer, airframe, and cement industry. Perhaps the most interesting hypothesis supported by empirical testing of this evolutionary model successor is that "technology evolves through relatively long periods of incremental change punctuated by relatively rare innovations that radically improve the state of the art. Such discontinuities occurred only eight times in the 190 total years observed across three industries."[10] This result is illustrated by performance trend data in the aircraft industry reproduced in Figure 60.[11]

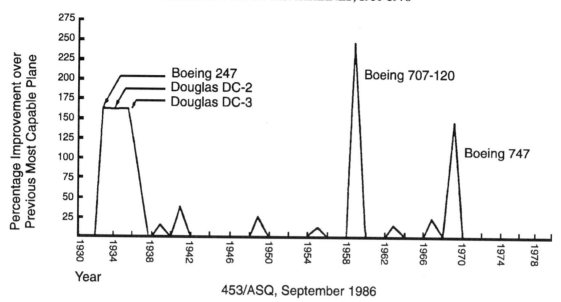

FIGURE 60
SEAT-MILES-PER-YEAR CAPACITY OF THE MOST CAPABLE
PLANE FLOWN BY U.S. AIRLINES, 1930-1978

453/ASQ, September 1986

Source: From Tushman and Anderson, 1986, p.453

Additionally, the authors found that when these major innovations do appear, competence-destroying discontinuities are initiated by new firms and competence-enhancing discontinuities are initiated by existing firms that are associated with decreased environmental turbulence. Firms that initiated major technological innovations were found to grow more rapidly than other firms.

There is no apparent, clear-cut successor to this most recent, punctuated equilibrium installment to the evolutionary theory of technological innovation, but it has been renamed as co-evolution and attracted more followers including Winter and others. However, one candidate is resource-based theory, which has attracted a great deal of attention and has been popularized by such works as Prahalad and Hammel's concept of core competence.

Resource-based Theory

Application of a resource-based view of the firm requires going beyond what economists typically include in this category: labor, capital, and land. A resource is defined as "anything which could be thought of as a strength or weakness of a given firm," and the fundamental question asked by the theory is "under what circumstances will a resource lead to high returns over longer periods of time?"

Products require the use of resources. New products often require new technology. In theory, it is possible to specify a resource profile of a firm and determine the optimal product-market activities. The more diversified the firm is or can become, the more useful such a theory is because it is a special case of the traditional theory of factor demand, but in this case, resources such as technological skills do not exhibit traditional properties in models such as declining returns to scale. An example of the theory is the economies of scope concept (Milgrom and Roberts).[12]

Taking technology as a special resource category raises several interesting derivative issues for resource-based theories. In particular, which technology should be the basis of diversification? A general proposition of the theory for large firms is that strategy involves "striking a balance between the exploitation of existing resources and the development of new ones." The theory can be developed to show when sequential entry into markets is desirable. For example, going international from a position of strength in a product and technological resources is desirable because it often occurs when the first (domestic) market is large relative to the second, when the second market uses less of the resources, or when the first product uses a lot of the first resource.

Challenges remain for resources-based theories. Products are relatively easy to identify as compared to resources, and how to combine resources across divisions is a chronic challenge for all complex organizations. Few if any firms have mastered technology-sharing schemes for best technology-resource allocation, and those that are successful have great difficulty achieving success over short periods of time.[13] Most successful firms seem to evolve this capability over longer periods of time like technology centers at Dow Chemical, which were first instituted there in 1965.

An excellent example of this proposition is given by Dierickx and Cool.[14] The authors argue that asset stock accumulation and sustainability are the key to competitive advantage. They cite the case of Canon versus Xerox corporation in the copier business. "Capitalizing on its stock of R&D, Canon was able to 'design service out of the product' thereby substituting superior product design for Xerox's extensive service network." With this substitution, Xerox's service network became somewhat obsolete, and customers defected.

Kazanjian and Drazin[15] tested and generally supported the stage of growth progression model for 71 technology-based new ventures in the computer and electronics industry. These firms generally progress from one to another of the four stages (conception and development, commercialization, growth, and stability) of growth in about 18 months. However, there are some noticeable exceptions to this pattern. Some firms regress, some move faster than predicted. This suggests a central tendency rather than a developmental imperative, and stage transition is also likely to be influenced by environment, structure, leadership and strategy. However, their overall discriminant analysis was significant and a total of 64 or 72% of the ventures were classified correctly (91% of stage 1 firms, 72% of stage 2 firms, 67% of stage 3 firms and 69% of stage 4 firms). This suggests the resource-based theory of the firm is robust enough to apply to rapidly growing firms.

Further to this point, Kogut and Zander[16] suggest that firms learn new skills by recombining their current capabilities, which might explain the transition between stages in the Kazanjian and Drazin[17] results. Growth occurs, Kogut and Zander[18] argue by building on social relationships that exist currently within the firm. This strongly supports the resource-based theory of the firm and suggests that the behavior of organizations is predictable from their past.

Chen and MacMillian[19] found that in a situation where the influence of corporate-business relationship on intra-industry competition is low, as in the U.S. airline industry, which is comprised of single or dominant industry firms, the attackers and responders to competitive moves gain share at the expense of nonresponders. However, the high incidence of nonresponse in their data (only 103 of 856 actions provoked at least one response) suggests more "serious attention should be paid to the resource-based view of firms...according to which, firm attributes, often idiosyncratic and thus nonimitable, may impede competitive responses."[20]

Revisiting Product-Process Dependencies

Although a resource-based approach has great appeal, it does not specifically inform the evolution or nature of product-product dependencies in organizations. Hage originally characterized all innovations is this sequence as either input, throughput, or output changes. If material (input) and process (throughput) innovations can be collapsed into one category for the purposes of this discussion, considerable enhancement of both the punctuated equilibrium and resource-based theories of innovation are needed before they will be useful as a guide to supply chain management.

At least one promising avenue of theoretical embellishment began with Daft's[21] dual-core theory of the innovation process, which was supported by data from school districts. Daft found that technological innovations originated from the technical core of organizations, and trickled up through the hierarchy. Administrative innovations originated in the administrative core of these units and trickled down. Administrative changes were more size independent but both innovations had significant implications for the functioning of these schools. However, dual-core theory does not specify the relationship between administrative and technological innovations.

Subsequent theoretical developments such as models of loose coupling (Weick[22] and Orton and Weick[23]) applied to organizational integration and the adoption of process technology (Ettlie and Reza[24]) provide new evidence that product-process dependencies are essential to understand in predicting the appropriation of innovation benefits. In particular, Ettlie and Reza studied over three dozen U.S. durable goods plants undergoing modernization and found that successful organizations use four integrating mechanisms of two types to capture value from process innovation. Findings supported the idea that three upstream integrating mechanisms directed at the valued-added chain — new hierarchical structure, increased coordination between design and manufacturing, and greater supplier cooperation — positively affect the productivity of new manufacturing systems, and one market-directed, downstream mechanism, forming new customer alliances, positively affects new system flexibility.

The impact of new processing technologies is not trivial. In spite of the fact that there have been some well-publicized failures of modernization programs at such large companies as General Motors Corporation during the 1980's, Ettlie and Reza found that when larger samples of firms are studied systematically using on-site collected data at these durable goods plants, quality performance alone, as measured by decreases in scrap and rework costs, improves *on average* by 30 percent. Furthermore, there has been a steady, nearly linear, uninterrupted increase in two-shift utilization of productive equipment in modernizing plants since 1969 (Ettlie and Reza[25]), averaging 1 percent per year, each year, and reaching of level of 72%, *on average,* in 1987-88. These data trends are summarized in Figure 61.

FIGURE 61
MANUFACTURING SYSTEM UTILIZATION RATES:
DOMESTIC PLANTS, SAMPLE SIZES VARY

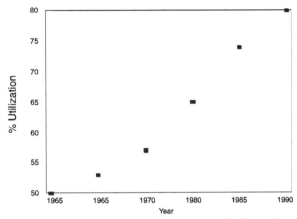

Other recent studies have reported very similar, impressive results from the application of new processing technology. For example, Swamidass[26] found that firms modernizing their operations had significantly higher sales per employee. "In a study I did recently with the National Association of Manufacturers in Washington, D.C., I found that in the average manufacturing plant conforming to selected industrial classifications (SIC 34 through 39), the sales per employee was US $141,000, while in plants using certain modern technologies it was nearly $200,000. The point is, technology is a proven source of productivity growth in manufacturing."[27]

Federal Reserve Bank of Chicago economists recently compiled the results of several academic studies on regional differences, which show that the "recent takeoff in Midwest manufacturing productivity can be traced directly to significant modernization efforts in several key industries."[28] Average capital expenditure per worker in the Midwest was 9 percent above the level elsewhere in the nation.... Manufacturing in the region improved efficiency by 8 percent more than corresponding sectors in the rest of the nation." This is particularly impressive given the mature industries like steel and autos that populate this region.

It is important to note that these are *average* increases in performance. More importantly, applied research on these issues is in the business of discovering the reasons for *variance* in performance. It is not so much the act of adoption that counts but the way in which technology is adopted and routinized. For example, Ettlie and Reza were able to account for a significant amount of variance in throughput time reduction, two-shift utilization, cycle-time achievement, scrap and rework reduction, and flexibility (part families) improvement by documenting administrative innovations used in conjunction with new process technology incorporation. Simultaneous design of new products and new production processes was an essential feature of this fabric of administrative innovations, significantly correlated with higher utilization of new production systems. Hierarchical integrating significantly enhanced throughput time reduction, and supplier integration significantly reduced scrap and rework and increased cycle time achieved with these new manufacturing systems.

This latter set of these integrating, administrative innovations, which have important implications for supplier management practices, is of special interest here. These new supply practices were adopted with the explicit intention of enhancing the probability of successful incorporation of process technology innovations, and they included the following, significantly:

1. Introduction of procedures for JIT (just-in-time) purchasing or delivery;

2. The adoption of new purchasing policies (e.g., "green purchasing agreements");

3. The purchase of integrated components;

4. Establishment of supplier education programs in such areas as SPC (statistical process control);*

5. Establishment of a contingency supply policy — for example, the identification of backup sources;

6. The reduction of inspection of incoming parts;

7. Installing supplier reward programs.

In many ways, these specific practices that distinguished successful process innovators from their peers are less important than the latent characteristic being modeled here: the relentless drive toward more control, simplification and rationalization of supply chain management — not only in supplier relations, but in product-process integration and hierarchical changes, as well, which impact throughput performance.

There are a number of emerging trends that are extrapolations of these administrative innovations and have significant implications for the next decade of supply chain management. These trends are taken up next in the final section of this paper.

Evolution of the Productive Segment and Supply Chain Management

The implications of organizational integration and evolution of the productive segment of the firm for supply chain management are potentially quite significant. In general, there appear to be linear, negative slope trends that show continued and dramatic decline in first-tier supply for most manufacturers. One example of these data is that which we collected for U.S. durable goods companies as part of the International Manufacturing Strategy Survey (IMSS).** In Figure 62,the frequency distribution of the change in the number of suppliers during the past five years reported by 26 American manufacturers is presented. The average change was a *reduction of nine suppliers (s.d.=25.8)*. In Figure 63, this same sample of 26 firms reports on the estimated change in the number of suppliers for the coming five years (1993-1998). Again, the average is a *reduction of nine suppliers (s.d.=37.5)*.

One interpretation of these trends is that this is the beginning of dramatic changes aimed at reducing the cost and complexity of value-added chain through persistent rationalization and sustainable innovative capability (Jelenik and Schoonhoven).[29] In particular, recent trends and the extrapolation of current theory and empirical observations suggest relentless technological and organizational transitions that appear to affect at least five issues in materials and supply chain management. These are taken up separately below.

Systems Philosophy of Operations

In several recent reports, one which included 16 research projects comparing U.S. and Japanese technology management practices, attention is being given to the importance of systems thinking in deployment of new technologies and achievement of additional performance gains by the synergistic impact of doing many things well. In case after case, successful companies seem to be able to coordinate the actions of several key functions and activities, often through teams, partnerships, and effective manufacturing strategies, to achieve the best results. In particular, the integration of the technological innovation and quality agenda of the business units of companies

---

* A total of 19 or 49 percent of plants studied by Ettlie and Reza had established such supplier education programs, similar to findings reported by Flynn and Cole for automotive suppliers.

** The IMSS survey is funded by the London Business School and Chalmers University. Data were collected from high-added value, U.S. firms during 1992-1993 (Ettlie, 1993).

FIGURE 62
CHANGE IN NUMBER OF SUPPLIERS IN LAST FIVE YEARS

Value	Frequency	Percent	Valid Percent	Cum Percent
-10	5	12.2	19.2	19.2
0	4	9.8	15.4	34.6
-25	3	7.3	11.5	46.2
10	3	7.3	11.5	57.7
-50	2	4.9	7.7	65.4
-20	2	4.9	7.7	73.1
-60	1	2.4	3.8	76.9
-30	1	2.4	3.8	80.8
-28	1	2.4	3.8	84.6
-15	1	2.4	3.8	88.5
20	1	2.4	3.8	92.3
25	1	2.4	3.8	96.2
65	1	2.4	3.8	100.0
-1	15	36.6	Missing	
Total	41	100.0	100.0	

Mean = -9.923   Mode = -10   Std Dev = 25.825

FIGURE 63
ESTIMATED CHANGE IN NUMBER OF SUPPLIERS IN NEXT FIVE YEARS

Value	Frequency	Percent	Valid Percent	Cum Percent
0	6	14.6	23.1	23.1
-50	3	7.3	11.5	34.6
-15	3	7.3	11.5	46.2
-10	3	7.3	11.5	57.7
-60	2	4.9	7.7	65.4
-25	2	4.9	7.7	73.1
-20	2	4.9	7.7	80.8
10	2	4.9	7.7	88.5
1	1	2.4	3.8	92.3
50	1	2.4	3.8	96.2
130	1	2.4	3.8	100.0
-1	15	36.6	Missing	
Total	41	100	100	

Mean = -9.000   Mode=000   Std Dev=37.534

appears to be a point of particular difference between successful and unsuccessful companies. In less successful **automotive companies, for example, technology decisions and quality improvements are not the responsibility of the same parts of the organization. In Japanese firms, everyone takes responsibility for both agendas (Cole).**[30] In a successful Japanese company, if any employee finds a good idea or practice outside the firm, he or she feels obligated to get this information to the correct person or persons for action and dissemination. The Japanese have adopted the eco-factory as one of the key focal points of the next decade, which follows naturally from their total quality control philosophy. Organizational learning is emphasized. Systemic action is of paramount importance.

Co-Production

When flexible or "joint" manufacturing of multiple products on a single production system was introduced during the 1970's, little did anyone know what strategic changes were afoot in plants everywhere and how the economies of scope would become a significant alternative to the economies of scale as a foundation theory of production (Milgrom and Roberts).[31] Now a new wave of "co-production" has begun to emerge, which may have an equally significant impact on production theory.

Examples of suppliers sharing production floor space with customers fully integrated into value-added productive operations are beginning to appear. Originally prevented by antitrust constraints, partners now pursue joint

81

optimization as needed to meet global competitive demands. An example is IBM's foray into joint production early in this decade in Europe and the Buick Reatta line in East Lansing during the same period.

The latter example of co-production was a partnership between PPG and General Motors Corporation. Cars become the complete charge of PPG employees when they entered the paint area. UAW employees who had temporary assignments in paint were exempt from contract rules. The original proposal for this arrangement was that PPG would actually buy the cars from GM, paint them, and then sell them back, but the co-productive alliance that resulted was never quite that extreme. However, this precedent for co-production and others has sweeping implications for supplier-customer relationships in a boundaryless organization of the future.

Reconciliation of Purchasing Policies

Current practice in U.S. manufacturing differentiates purchasing policies for materials, components, and technology. Although the advent of "black box" sourcing in the automotive industry, which allows suppliers to maximize return on R&D expenditures for integrated components, appears to be a solid trend with little change during the next decade, the purchase of new technology for processing and other purchasing arrangements still tends to be covered by different policies. Black box purchasing seems to have influenced this current practice very little — it is merely an outgrowth of component purchases of the past.

It seems reasonable to predict that eventually, the pressure to integrate and rationalize purchasing will require reconciliation of these various policies. Opportunities for experimentation abound. For example, in one recent green field modernization site of an engine component supplier and division of one of the Big Three automotive OEMs, commodity purchasing was contracted out, and small firm supplier rules (minimum size of supplier resource base) was set aside in order that the best (in this case, domestic) machine tool supplier be allowed to do business on the project. The integrating principle was not precedent or current policy and practice, but what was needed to maximize supplier responsiveness. More of these experiments are on the horizon.

One area where significant innovation is beginning to occur on this front is in firm relationships with universities (see supply chain integration below for an example). In particular, the arm's-length relationship of past, in which the students or graduates were the only link between firms and universities, is slowly giving way to a more European or Japanese model of direct connections through contract research and consulting on major projects with faculty which is supported by comparative research.

Commenting on several comparative studies of national innovation systems, Winter (1993) says, "One important feature distinguishing countries that were sustaining competitive and innovative firms was education and training systems that provide these firms with a flow of people with the requisite knowledge and skills. For industries in which university-trained engineers and scientists were needed, this does not simply mean that the universities provide training in these fields, but also that they consciously train their students with an eye to industry needs." The establishment of government-sponsored centers at universities like the NSF programs and others appears to have had a great impact on these new relationships.

Winter further reports that where public or university labs seem to help in promoting innovativeness of national firms, the trend is toward "direct interactions between particular firms and particular faculty members or research projects, as through consulting arrangements . . . . "

Manufacturing Strategies and Purchasing-Design Consolidation

As many as 80 percent of the parts of old products are used in new products. The new Honda Accord and Ford Mustang have significant part overlap. As products gradually improve, more old design parts can be used in times of even greater resource constraints. But even in this consolidated environment of world-wide design integration, Ford Motor Company still does not have an integrated purchasing and design data base or software to use these data.

As a consequence of the growing interest in articulating and formalizing manufacturing strategies (Voss[32]), and proposals for mechanisms of technology sharing (Rubenstein[33]), various essential decisions for future operations are likely to force an integration of design and purchasing. In the past, make-buy decisions were often made independently of modernization investments, product planning decisions, and technology acquisition choices. These types of uncoordinated practices are for less successful companies.

Integration and Consolidation of Supply Chain Management

The simplification and continued integration and consolidation of supply chain management through reduction of the number of first-tier suppliers and such methods as JIT II (which has been implemented at Bose and other companies) seems to be just around the corner. What Bose has done is to replace the supplier sales representative, customer purchasing agent, and production scheduler with an "in-plant" supplier representative. Orders are released by suppliers when customer demand becomes known, effectively eliminating three jobs in the supply chain.

A unique variant on this theme is a recent University of Michigan student project under the MAP (Multidisciplinary Action Projects) and the MJMI (Michigan Joint Manufacturing Initiative) internship program. With AlliedSignal, an order-to-remittance reengineering project was successfully initiated at several locations, with particular success at one southern plant (video available). This joint university-industry project represents not only the new rationalization of the value-added chain but a unique experience that promotes organizational learning in both institutions.

Winter reports that a number of cases verify the proposition that "firms in industries where a country is strong tend to have strong interactive linkages with their upstream suppliers, who are also national firms . . . . The supplier networks of Japanese automobile firms, and the upstream/downstream connections of Danish agricultural product processing, are good examples. The cooperation of Italian textile producers with each other and with their equipment suppliers is another." Winter also reports that the pharmaceutical and aircraft production industries appear to be exceptions to this trend.

In summary, there are five predicted trends in evolution of the productive segment that have implications for materials and supply chain management.

1. Systemic thinking: In particular the **convergence of the technology and quality (including the ecofactory) agenda** of the business unit.

2. Joint production (i.e., flexibility and economies of scope) are likely to be enhanced by **co-production:** the actual sharing of productive facilities between suppliers and users.

3. The merging or conscious **reconciliation of supplier policies** for technology and component or service purchase. This includes a much more sophisticated approach to dealing with universities.

4. The integration of purchase and engineering design data base management systems as part of greater emphasis on articulating and implementing **manufacturing strategies.**

5. The simplification and continued **integration and consolidation of supply chain** management through reduction of the number of first-tier suppliers and use of such methods such as JIT II and other mechanisms (e.g., AlliedSignal's order-to-remittance reengineering project) that promote a learning organization.

Each one of these trends and many more not covered in this paper (e.g., 24-hour production; global manufacturing; and rapid product realization) reflect this endless quest for a finish line that does not exist in operations. Only continuous improvement is considered a sustainable philosophy today. These trends are dominated by technological innovation and rationalization through integration and simplification. The details seem less important, but the reality of these trends is already upon us.

References

1. Abernathy, W.J. and Wayne, 1974, "Limits of the Learning Curve."

2. Abernathy, W.J. and Townsend, P.L. 1975, "Technology, Productivity, and Process Change," *Technological Forecasting and Social Change*, Vol. 7, 379-396.

3. Utterback, J.M. and Abernathy, W.J., 1975, "A Dynamic Model of Process and Product Innovation," *Omega*, Vol. 3, No. 6, 639-656.

4. Abernathy, W.J., 1976, "Production Process Structure and Technological Change," *Decision Sciences,* Vol. 7, No. 4 607-619.

5. Utterback, J.M. and Abernathy, W.J., 1975, "A Dynamic Model of Process and Product Innovation," *Omega,* Vol. 3, No. 6, 639-656.

6. Utterback, J.M. and Abernathy, W.J., 1975, "A Dynamic Model of Process and Product Innovation," *Omega,* Vol. 3, No. 6, 642.

7. Utterback, J.M. and Abernathy, W.J., 1975, "A Dynamic Model of Process and Product Innovation," *Omega,* Vol. 3, No. 6, 639-656.

8. Ettlie, J.E., 1979, "Evolution of the Productive Segment and Transportation Innovations," *Decision Sciences,* Vol. 10, No. 3, 399-411.

9. Tushman, M.L. and Anderson, P., 1986, "Technological Discontinuities and Organizational Environments," *Administrative Science Quarterly,* Vol. 31, 439-465.

10. Tushman, M.L. and Anderson, P., 1986, "Technological Discontinuities and Organizational Environments," *Administrative Science Quarterly,* Vol. 31, 460.

11. Tushman, M.L. and Anderson, P., 1986, "Technological Discontinuities and Organizational Environments," *Administrative Science Quarterly,* Vol. 31, 453.

12. Milgrom, P. and Roberts, J., 1990, "The Economics of Modern Manufacturing: Technology, Strategy, and Organization," *American Economic Review,* Vol. 80, 511-528.

13. Rubenstein, A.H., 1989, *Managing Technology in the Decentralized Firm,* New York, Wiley Interscience.

14. Dierickx, I. and Cool, K. "Asset Stock Accumulation and Sustainability of Competitive Advantage," *Management Science,* Vol. 35, No. 12, 1504-1514.

15. Kazanjian, R.K. and Drazin, R., 1989, "An Empirical Test of a Stage of Growth Progression Model," *Management Science,* Vol. 35, No. 12, 1489-1503.

16. Kogut, B. and Zander, U., 1992, "Knowledge of the Firm, Combinative Capabilities, and the Replication of Technology," *Organization Science,* Vol. 3, No. 3, 383-397.

17. op. cit.

18. op. cit.

19. Chen, M. and MacMillan, I., 1992, "Nonresponse and Delayed Response to Competitive Moves: The Roles of Competitor Dependence and Action Irreversibility," *Academy of Management Journal,* Vol. 35, No. 3, 539-570.

20. Chen, M. and MacMillan, I., 1992, "Nonresponse and Delayed Response to Competitive Moves: The Roles of Competitor Dependence and Action Irreversibility," *Academy of Management Journal,* Vol. 35, No. 3, 568.

21. Daft, R.L., 1978, "A Dual-Core Model of Organizational Innovation," *Academy of Management Journal,* Vol. 21, 193-210.

22. Weick, K.E., 1976, "Educational Organizations as Loosely Coupled Systems," *Administrative Science Quarterly,* Vol. 21, 1-19.

23. Orton, J.D. and Weick, K.E., 1990, "Loosely Coupled Systems: A Reconceptualization," *Academy of Management Review,* Vol. 15, 203-233.

24. Ettlie, J.E. and Reza, 1992, "Organizational Integration and Process Innovation," *Academy of Management Journal,* Vol. 35, No. 4, 795-827.

25. op. cit.

26. Swamidass, P.M., 1993, "Technology. People, and Management," *IEEE Spectrum,* Vol. 30, No. 9, 68-69.

27. Swamidass, P.M., 1993, "Technology. People, and Management," *IEEE Spectrum,* Vol. 30, No. 9, 69.

28. *Business Week*, October 18, 1993, p. 18.

29. Jelenik, M. and Schoonhoven, C., 1990, *The Innovation Marathon,* Oxford, England: Basil Blackwell, Ltd.

30. Cole, R., 1990, "U.S. Quality Improvement in the Auto Industry: Close But No Cigar," *California Management Review,* Summer, 71-85.

31. op. cit.

32. Voss, C., 1993 (September 23), Personal Communication, London Business School, England.

33. op. cit.

COMPETITIVE DIRECTIONS IN PURCHASING
Harold Fearon, Ph.D.
Center For Advanced Purchasing Studies

This presentation traces the evolution of the Purchasing function from a managerial orientation to a strategic orientation in recent years. Current trends are enumerated and future trends are identified. The presentation concludes by identifying opportunities that exist in Purchasing.

I. How Has the Purchasing Function Evolved?

  1. 1900 to 1939

  2. Effects of World War II

  3.   Managerial Emphasis (1950s and 1960s)

  4. Strategic Beginnings (1970s and 1980s)

  5. 1985 - Present

      A. Changing Technology

      B. Competitive Pressures in Many Industries

      C. Worldwide Markets

      D. Downsizing, Rightsizing, Reengineering

II. Trends Now Under Way in Purchasing/Materials Management

  1. Total Quality and Customer Satisfaction Emphasis

  2. Emphasis on Process, not Transactions

  3. Purchasing Becomes Contracting; Scheduling and Expediting Done Elsewhere

  4. Design Engineering and Purchasing Synergy

  5. Supplier Base Reformulated

  6. Longer-Term Contracts

  7. EDI with Major Suppliers

  8. MRO Items Handled by Third Party

  9. Sourcing Includes Complete End Product and Done Offensively

  10. Development of Integrated Suppliers/Partners

  11. Closer Supplier Relationships

  12. Empowerment

III. Trends in Purchasing/Materials Management in the Next Decade

1. Integration into Business Strategy

2. Supply Chain Management

3. End Product Manufacturers Focus on Design and Assembly

4. Procurement and Manufacturing Cycles Reduced

5. Transport Decisions Become Buyer Responsibility

6. Functional Lines Blurred or Eliminated

7. Teaming Used To Achieve Business Objectives

8. "Pull Systems" Prevail in Manufacturing

9. Networking of Suppliers

10. Reduction of Third- and Fourth-Tier Suppliers

11. Evaluation Factors Change in International Purchases

12. Technical Entry Route into Purchasing

13. Nontraditional People in Purchasing Management

14. Systems and Services Purchases More Important

15. Tiers of Purchasing People

IV. Current Issues/Problems, and Opportunities

1. Little Change: Most organizations have not changed significantly their purchasing process over the last 20 to 30 years.

2. Clerical Role: Purchasing still regarded as primarily a clerical activity in most organizations.

3. Little Involvement in Nontraditional Buying: Purchasing departments focus primarily on buying goods and services. Most departments have little input into buying decisions on capital equipment, transportation, resale items, services, construction, utilities, or real estate. If purchasing has a process or expertise, why is it largely ignored?

4. Developmental Position: In many leading-edge companies, the top purchasing position is regarded as a developmental experience on the way to some other executive position within the organization.

5. Few University Programs: There are few fully accredited university undergraduate degree programs in purchasing/materials management and almost no master degree programs; purchasing coverage is almost absent in most of the nationally-rated M.B.A. programs.

6. Few Faculty: Relatively few regular faculty members have their primary academic interest in purchasing/materials management.

7. Little College Recruiting: There is relatively little corporate on-campus recruiting of university graduates to enter purchasing.

8. <u>Measurement Systems Lacking</u>: We still do not have good measurement/evaluation systems for purchasing effectiveness, and that which we don't measure doesn't get much attention. What measurements do purchasing professionals need to improve performance? What measurements does top management want or need?

9. <u>Top Management Doubts Effectiveness</u>: Most top management (presidents/CEOs) feel the purchasing function is very important, but many feel it is only moderately effective. Is this partly because believable metrics are lacking?

10. <u>Little Contribution to Corporate Strategy</u>: Purchasing is not a major contributor to key corporate areas of strategy development, economic forecasting, long-term planning, product innovation, technological development, and market planning.

11. <u>Risk-Taking not Expected</u>: Presidents/CEOs feel that purchasing contributes by assuring supply, containing prices, and maintaining ethical standards. They are not expected to take risk, innovate, or assure external customer satisfaction. If purchasing maintains a "play-it-safe" approach, will the potential be realized?

**Changing Manufacturing Management
& Technology:
Implications for Purchasing Futures**
Chan K. Hahn, Ph.D.
NAPM Professor
Bowling Green State University

Environmental Forces Causing Changes

1. Low Growth/Mature Market very volatile for individual industry/company.

2. Globalization of Market/Competition — global market intense competition from many international sources technological as well as cost competition, global economic activities (Figure 64).

FIGURE 64
ENVIRONMENTAL FORCES CAUSING CHANGES IN MANUFACTURING AND PURCHASING

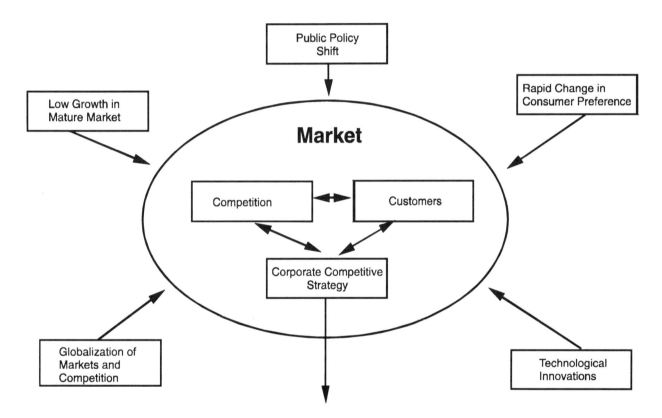

3. Changing Consumer Preference diversified consumer needs (customization) large variety with small volume, faster services, demand for higher quality at low-cost design flexibility (Figure 65).

4. Technological Innovations — product innovations, process capability improvement, shorter lead time/new product introduction, shorter product life cycle.

5. Public Policy deregulations NATA, EC, APEC, U. Round Federal Deficit

Impact on Manufacturing Management

The new market/competitive structure demands vastly different performance from manufacturing managers in terms of quality, delivery, cost, and flexibility (Figure 66).

FIGURE 65
SHIFTING MANUFACTURING STRATEGY

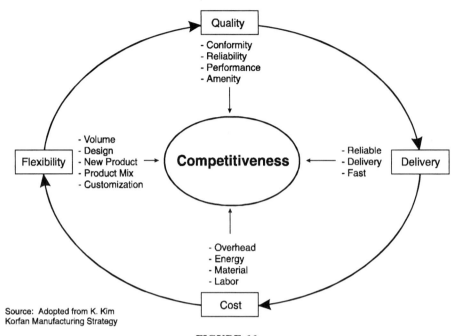

Source: Adopted from K. Kim
Korfan Manufacturing Strategy

FIGURE 66
CORPORATE MANUFACTURING AND PURCHASING STRATEGIES

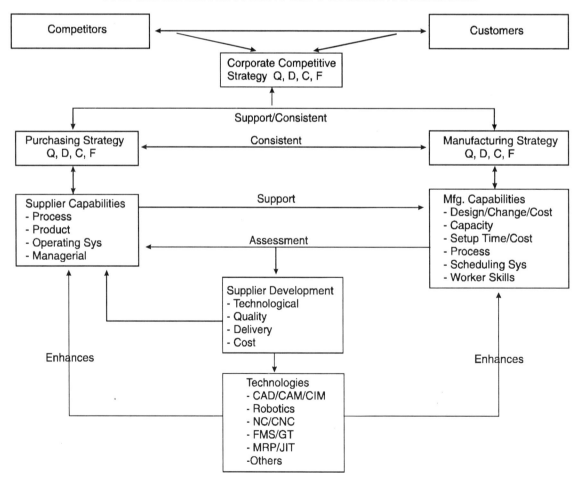

Manufacturing must emphasize:

1. Capability to introduce new product quickly.

2. Capability to quickly respond to customer request in terms of design change of customized product request.

3. Versatile process capability
   Flexible low cost automation.

4. Capability to adopt new technology quickly.

5. Operating systems to handle the variations.

6. Better trained/skilled work force.

7. Competent supplier network.

Implications for Purchasing/Materials Management

1. Shifting Paradigm for Supplier Relationship (Figure 67).

FIGURE 67
SHIFTING PARADIGM FOR SUPPLIER RELATIONSHIP

	Basis for Supplier Selection	
	Product/Commodity Based	Capability Based

Adversarial
 	
Bargaining Power
Relationship
 	
Buyer's   Seller's
    >
Power   Power
	- Short-term/Tactical Emphasis
	- Price Reduction Based on Bargaining
	- Multiple Sourcing
	  (competition emphasis) =>
	- Conformance Quality
	  (emphasis)
		- Long-term/Strategic Emphasis
		- Negotiated Price
		
		- Competitive Multiple Sourcing
		- Reliability Quality

Cooperative
 	
Partnership-Like
 	
Buyer's   Seller's
    =
Power   Power
	- Longer-term/Tactical Emphasis
	- Nonprice Based
	
	- Technical Assistance for
	  Quality Improvement =>
	- Management Assistance
	- Supplier Development
	
	- Reduced Supplier Base
		- Strategic Emphasis
		
		- Cost Reduction Through
		  Continuous Improvement
		- Single Sourcing
		
		- Technical Cooperation
		- Performance Quality
		  Emphasis

2. Organizational Structure/Control - more centralized control for strategic issues decentralized format for operational issues cross-functional team work flexible/modular more frequent job rotation.

3. Purchasing Information/Technology - real-time information system (progress report) networking/EDP must be able to handle wider variety of information.

4. Supplier Relations supplier development emphasis Keiretsu-type relationship.

5. Training and Education - broader definition of body of knowledge, continuing education is critical to keep up with rapid changes, need for professional standards.

6. Research issues dealing with new paradigm implications of more integrated purchasing function.

SOME THOUGHTS ABOUT THE FUTURE OF THE PURCHASING/MATERIALS MANAGEMENT/LOGISTICS ENVIRONMENT IN YEAR 2001

Thomas Hendrick, Ph.D.
Arizona State University
Center for Advanced Purchasing Studies

- Purchasing/materials management/logistics as identifiable "functional silos" will have become "blurred" as they are more fully integrated through multidisciplined commodity "sourcing teams" to design and manage demand-supply chains.

- On-line information/decision support systems will allow fewer cross-disciplined technically and business-trained sourcing teams to effectively manage a drastically reduced supply base through a centralized/decentralized organizational structure.

- Building and managing strategic supply-base "relationships" will consume almost all of the time of sourcing teams, while day-to-day operational transactions will be delegated to internal customers, key suppliers, and automated expert decision systems using artificial intelligence methods.

- Outsourcing of materials and services will continue to increase, and will include services heretofore thought not to be strong candidates for outsourcing — such as purchasing, personnel, and quality management. In addition, more value-added services relating to materials will be assumed by the supplier base.

- Commodities traditionally not managed by purchasing (health care, financial services, consulting, training, transportation) will be managed by sourcing teams.

- Organization-wide initiatives for processes' time compression and synchronization of processes for product/service design, procurement, production/operations, distribution, and supporting administrative functions will become as important as the current movements of total customer satisfaction and TQM/CQI.

- Buyer-supplier partnering/alliances will endure as a major strategic initiative and encompass the entire demand-supply chain, including second-level, third-level (perhaps beyond) suppliers. Both parties will work to make the relationships "seamless," and continued associations will depend upon joint continuous improvement and shared risks and rewards.

- Value-added performance measurement of P/MM/L functions based on total cost of acquisition and ownership (TCAO) will be routinely measured through automated TCAO models whose results will dominate "price" as the primary sourcing decision variable. Top management will endorse this approach and will include it as an integral part of total strategic planning.

- Graduate higher education directed towards strategic P/MM/L demand-supply chain design and management will have taken root in ten AACSB universities and be recognized as an important discipline by world-class companies.

- The number of CEOs in *Fortune* 500 companies who have risen to the top through purchasing will increase.

FROM PURCHASING TO
MANAGING EXTERNAL OPERATIONS

Michiel R. Leenders, D.B.A.
The University of Western Ontario
and
Jean Nollet, Ph.D.
École des Hautes Études Commerciales de Montréal

Introduction

In the decade ahead the acquisition of goods and services will move out of purchasing's domain. Like customers, suppliers will be considered everyone's business.

If the purchasing function is to contribute effectively to organiztional goals and strategies, its practitioners will have to give up most of their hard-won territorial rights and become fully integrated into the customer-employer supplier chain. The view that purchasing is a service function is no longer useful.

A Sports Comparison

Imagine yourself as a fan at a sporting event 10 years from now. As the public address announcer introduces the teams, you find a number of your favorite players have disappeared and their places have been taken by contract players, many of whom you recognize as players on other teams and in other sports as well. Moreover, after the teams have been announced, the next message sends you into further confusion. "For this game the following rule and equipment changes are in effect."

In a sports context this may sound a bit farfetched, but in business and government this is exactly what is happening. And the implications for the effective management of supply are staggering.

Occasionally, in sports, some professional athletes are so talented as to achieve star status in more than one sport. An athlete like Bo Jackson can, for example, be a good baseball and football player. In these rare instances, it is interesting to see the concerns of the coaches and managers of the two different teams as they worry about injuries, season overlap, and divided loyalties. Coaches and managers are used to the team concepts where every player is exclusively engaged.

In business and government, the team concept is altering radically. Ideas like core business, downsizing, and outsourcing have drastically changed the composition of the team. Furthermore, customer satisfaction, empowerment, total quality management, total costs of ownership and cycle time reduction, flexibility, and the learning organisation have changed the responsibilities of the players.

In the sports context, in the successful organizations of the future we will be trying to play with a team where at least half of the players are not really on the team and where the rules have changed drastically. Few of today's sports managers and coaches would be comfortable in that environment. Not surprisingly, the challenge is equally great for managers in the nonsports environment.

In this article we explore the major implications of these changes for the purchasing function and how the nature of its contribution will have to change. First, the traditional service image of the function needs to be altered. Second, the purchasing manager will have to become a manager of external operations.

Purchasing's Traditional Service Image

The traditional view of purchasing has cast it in a service role. To stay with a sports perspective, purchasing has been the provider of towels, uniforms, and drinks for the team. This allowed the function to bask in the glory of the winning team, but the contribution, in truth, was minimal. The future perspective will require purchasing to be a player on the field contributing to the team's mission to win in every way possible. And suppliers will also have to be on the team.

For too long now most purchasing professionals have seen themselves as managing a service function: "We support operations, marketing, engineering, R&D, MIS, special programs and projects, etc." This perspective has been, rather uncritically, accepted for decades and not without reason. Let us examine what is right and what is wrong with this view.

What Is Right About the Service Perspective?

The usefulness of the service perspective has been its reinforcement that acquisition needs generated elsewhere in the organization had to be satisfied. The famous: "The right goods and services of the right quality and in the right quantity at the right time and the right place with the right services and support at the right 'price'" has been imprinted on every supply novice in every introductory course in the field.

This view reinforced the internal customer satisfaction perspective, a most useful reminder as to whose budget ultimately provided the funds for the acquisition.

The service perspective also fit the notion that separation is required between those who specify acquisition requirements, those who use what is required, those who purchase and those who pay. Keeping these four groups apart served the financial and audit requirements with respect to misappropriation of funds. As long as these four groups did not get too close, the possibilities of fraud would be minimized.

This perspective also gave the acquisition function a reasonable amount of independence. Not many in the organization cared how purchases were done as long as they received what they wanted and, if possible, from whom they wanted it. The primary interest of auditors, aside from the prevention of fraud, centered on procedural compliance rather than value for money spent.

Some of the more enterprising practitioners viewed their relative independence as an opportunity to experiment and widen the boundaries of the field. It is this latter aspect that has been the best outcome from this period of clutching to the service perspective. An impressive body of knowledge, full of theoretical tools, concepts and skills has been built up over the years, leading to the professionalization of the purchasing manager.

An appropriate conclusion is that the service perspective has probably been a useful and necessary stage in the evolution of the profession.

What Is Wrong with the Service Perspective?

The key problem with the traditional service perspective for purchasing is that it prevents the profession from moving where the future demands that it go.

The traditional service perspective puts the acquisition area into a box, a territory in which requisitions come in through the hole in the near wall and purchase orders go out through the hole in the far wall. More territorial battles have taken place over even this territory as others tried to bypass the organizational policy that "Purchasing Must Purchase" or "Supplier Selection Is Purchasing's Responsibility." Numerous marketing studies have shown that multiple influencers exist for every purchase. Proper supplier selection is impossible without appropriate recognition of the stakeholders involved.

Ideas like value analysis, standardization, and simplification, some of the simplest and yet most powerful value improvement tools in the supply area, could never be fully exploited in the service context. These tools required too many inputs from outside the "box" and at the same time were not seen as sufficiently service-oriented.

Over two decades ago Dean Ammer tried very hard to interest materials managers and accountants in accepting the idea of materials management as a profit center. Reluctance of both materials and accounting professionals to give serious consideration to this (at the time) revolutionary idea was certainly one obstacle he faced.

The long-standing paradigm has been that the budget responsibility of the materials manager was to be focused on the cost of running the materials department. The cost of materials and services acquired were meant to be part of other people's budgets and their bottom line responsibility. What was lost in the quick dismissal of Dean Ammer's ideas was the prime purpose for his suggestion. He was not particularly interested in starting an accounting debate.

He wanted to give bottom line responsibilities to materials management. He felt that too many improvement opportunities were missed because of the service perspective.

There are, of course, a number of additional problems with the service perspective. It puts purchasing into a chronology that favours sequential rather than simultaneous action, thereby adding time delays and missing opportunities for early supplier involvement.

The service perspective reduces the need for staffing with high quality personnel, since opportunities for strategic or bottom line improvement are seen as minimal. The focus on internal, rather than external customers also has potential dangers. It is easy to lose sight of the real external customers' needs, assuming that satisfying internal customers is sufficient.

The net outcome of the negative side of the service context for purchasing is that supply strategy is defined as dealing with specific suppliers or requirements, potentially without congruence with the organization's external customer needs and organizational objectives and strategies.

For any organization to be world class, its supply function will have to be world class and its major suppliers world class. That will require the supply function to be both operational as well as strategic in its contribution. And supply contribution must not only have direct impact on the bottom line, but also indirect impact in terms of enhancing the performance of others in the organization. It is exactly this perspective on the required contribution by the function that renders the service perspective obsolete.

From Purchasing to Managing External Operations

The strategic contribution required of supply in the future is based on the following conviction: *Suppliers and the way we relate to them must provide a competitive edge.* As long as purchasing is focused on selecting the best value option from a number of different bidders, presumably any other purchaser has exactly the same right and opportunity. As more and more organizations have turned to outsourcing and concentrating on their core business, the need to gain a competitive edge on the supply side has increased substantially.

A different approach to suppliers will require a different type of internal relationship between supply and the other functional areas as well. Managing the supplier relationship more effectively will require purchasing to relinquish its traditional gatekeeping role in communications with suppliers. Internal teamwork will become a prerequisite for external teamwork with customers and suppliers.

It is not surprising that, in manufacturing firms, the first tentative steps to internal functional teamwork came from trying to pressure new product design and manufacturing engineering to cooperate better. It must be a great surprise to outsiders that design for manufacturability should even be a challenge. And yet, it has been and still is. To achieve internal cooperation between marketing, operations, finance, human resources, engineering, accounting, and MIS is obviously a much larger feat.

To get the external customer recognized as an additional member of the team adds a totally new dimension. Is sales or marketing not supposed to take care of the external customer?

And, finally, this article insists that suppliers (and their suppliers) are also a significant part of the chain. David Burt and Michael Doyle reinforced this idea in their latest text. For too long many organizations have made the mistake of assuming that only sales and marketing should talk to external customers. However, are customers not everyone's concern? Similarly, suppliers should not be entrusted to purchasing alone. Suppliers, also, should be everyone's business.

Purchasing is going to have to open up the gateway to suppliers so that all other business functions can communicate directly with their appropriate counterparts in the suppliers' organizations. In far too many organizations sales/marketing and purchasing have effectively blocked access to customers and suppliers.

Sales/marketing and purchasing are referred to in the academic literature as boundary spanning functions, presumably because of their simultaneous internal and external contacts. In reality, every function will have to be boundary-spanning. The various attempts by organizations to create strategic alliances, preferred suppliers, single source and partnering types of arrangements with suppliers can be seen to contribute in two ways. First, they are an attempt to unlock benefits and create synergies not attainable in the standard arm's-length, competitive, non-trusting mode. Second, they may be seen as an attempt to substitute for internal relations lost due to outsourcing, and necessary for corporate success. Cooperative agreements with suppliers require far more in terms of top management and interfunctional contact within the purchasing organization as well as across the peer functions in the supplier's organization. It is very difficult for a cooperative buyer-supplier relationship to flourish without effective cooperation and teamwork inside the buyer's organization. Getting more from suppliers will require a different approach and structure internally.

Organizational Design Implications

The logical extension of these ideas into organizational design brings the following conclusion. Continuing to think of purchasing as a service function that can be assigned to any senior manager willing to take responsibilities is dysfunctional. Since operations have been basically split into internal and external segments, the supply manager should be considered as manager of external operations.

This new title does not suggest that the person in charge of external operations works in a closed-in box. Both the person in charge of internal operations, and the one in charge of the external operations will have to work closely together and with the other's functions, customers, and suppliers to ensure that opportunities for gaining competitive advantage are fully explored. The manager of external operations will have to focus on building links to ensure that the organizations' objectives are satisfactorily met.

Conclusion

In this article we have argued that the service perspective of purchasing has been useful in the past but no longer serves organizational goals well. Purchasing will have to become a regular player on the team, rather than a provider of towels, uniforms, and drinks. Key suppliers will also have to join the team. And the growing reliance on suppliers to provide goods and services formerly sourced internally is placing new demands on effective supply management. The purchasing manager should become a manager of external operations.

New Manufacturing Directions*

Jeffrey G. Miller, Ph.D.
Professor of Operations Management, Boston University
and
Dan Ciampa
President & CEO, Rath & Strong

American manufacturing managers have made tremendous strides over the last ten years. They have led the way in their corporations into Total Quality (TQ), increased the productivity of American manufacturing firms at a faster rate than their counterparts in Japan and Germany, and cut time out of processes. But these accomplishments offer little solace to those looking at what they must now achieve. Almost overnight, manufacturing has found itself in the midst of a new era in which it is being asked to fundamentally redefine its role. This era was not heralded by a clarion call like Total Quality; it has emerged as a consequence of the success in this and other initiatives, and from the ever increasing competition for the customer's favor.

The key manufacturing task in the new era is to create and seize business opportunities. This means doing things in manufacturing that create markets, capture new customers, and secure sustainable advantages over competitors. This is not business as usual, as Bill, the V.P. of Manufacturing for a major telecommunications manufacturer found out when he was asked to review his organization's accomplishments with the Chairman of his company. He and his organization had worked hard to improve manufacturing performance. They had reduced quality costs substantially, cut the time from order entry to delivery from 120 days to 20 days, and reduced overall manufacturing costs from 30 percent to 12 percent of sales. He was taken aback when the Chairman said at the completion of his review, "You've done a good job of taking time and cost out of manufacturing, but what has this given us that's of strategic value?" In manufacturing's current new era, it's assumed that any manufacturing executive worth his or her salt can improve quality, cost and timeliness — the new requirement is to help convert these accomplishments into business opportunity.

Trends In Government/Service Sector Purchasing
or
Completing the Metamorphosis
Stanley N. Sherman, Ph.D.
The George Washington University

Change in the workplace affects every management discipline. It appears to be an accelerating process derived from the broader spectrum of technical and societal changes that have mesmerized the world since the end of the Second World War. Many dramatic changes are only emerging during this decade, but it is becoming clear that the process is driven by communications and information technologies together with the opening of societies to wider exchange of ideas, products, and services. We seek a clearer vision of the product of change as it affects managers of purchasing, as the twentieth century draws to a close.

For government procurement, the peculiarities of the political process and regulatory reactions reduce, but do not eliminate, our ability to anticipate the composition of the federal purchasing environment, given a five-year time horizon.

Our concern in this conference is how change affects management disciplines, particularly the management of purchasing by organizations. I do not think we want to place purchasers in a management class by themselves; rather they should be considered as one group in the tableau of groups of dedicated professionals. Nor should we classify government buyers as a unique group. Purchasers are competing for recognition along with every fellow professional group. This competition is particularly keen among the emerging disciplines — those whose capabilities were masked by the higher priority given during earlier periods to science, engineering, marketing, finance, and production. Members of the emerging disciplines include managers of purchasing, quality, logistics, and materials. The traditionally recognized fields of activity continue to be vital, but the emerging management disciplines are taking the spotlight primarily because they may offer the greatest leverage for improvement and advancement in the 1990s.

Recognizing that competition among management groups may be an important reality, we should focus on their cooperation and collaboration. The profile of successful leaders in the twenty-first century is likely to be composed of members of teams and of the teams themselves. Their objective will be to create effective work processes, considering the interests and perceptions of the members of all relevant functions, including those defined as customers. This is most likely to be achieved when the affected groups work as teams. Consequently, the functional identification of underlying disciplines is less significant than the coordination of processes that make the organization a success.

I will spotlight three developments and trends that I consider vital to the future of purchasing whether in government or private sector organizations. They are the adoption of ISO 9000, the reworked governmental perception and regulation of purchasing, and the broadened scope of buyer responsibilities.

ISO 9000

Total quality management (TQM) is widely recognized as the best model, perhaps the only model, adequate to meet the demands of today's world-wide competitive environment. Nothing short of world-class management practices will be victorious in that environment. Unfortunately, many who speak about TQM are not clear as to how to bring it about. The idea itself has been demonstrated amply by its creators — Deming, Juran, Crosby and others. But a practical implementation methodology understandable to all has not been a part of broad-based developments to date. I suggest that ISO 9000 has created that methodology. Purchasing professionals, whether in government or industry, have an exceptional opportunity to become central figures in the developments that are at our threshold today.

Purchasers who will assume a leading role in promoting ISO 9000 must examine the concept, the objective, and the detailed requirements to the point that they comprehensively and intimately comprehend its full scope. The opportunity presented to purchasers by ISO 9000 is derived from the concept that ensures that anyone who buys a product or service can rely upon the supplier's promises with confidence that what is received will be what was expected. The opportunity is present, but reality also includes a caution that it would be inconsistent for purchasers to impose ISO 9000 obligations on their suppliers if they find their own organization cannot pass muster under the standards. It is fundamental that ISO 9000 qualification is a CEO commitment. All others in the organization must then participate.* Nevertheless, selling the idea of such commitment might originate anywhere in the organization, and purchasers who want visibility and status have a built-in advantage in being positioned to deal directly with suppliers.

The factors summarized in the following comments lead me to conclude that ISO 9000 standards are vitally important to the future of U. S. purchasers (and their employers, including government organizations).

1. ISO 9000 codifies common sense, it is not a set of new rules. It is focused on productive systems, asserts principles to ensure that the systems meet the expectations of customers, organizes the essential elements into 20 topics, and provides a basis for validation that an organization will produce quality output.

2. The ISO 9000 series of quality standards was published by the International Standards Organization (ISO) in 1987. The series was adopted by the European Community without change and is published as the European Norm (EN) 29000 series.

3. Most aspects of the ISO 9000 series were derived from U.S. military quality standards published in the 1950s. The most comprehensive of the standards, ISO 9001, is similar to Mil-Q-9858A, which is still in effect.

4. Qualification under ISO 9000 is voluntary under ISO rules but has become mandatory under certain circumstances by action of the European Community or by other specific governmental actions. Qualification must be accomplished by and at the expense of the company (or agency) seeking to be qualified.

5. Registration under ISO 9000 is distinguishable from qualification. Registration requires validation of the company's quality systems by an independent third party whose registry mark is recognized by contemporaries. The process of qualification refers to the steps taken by companies to ensure that their systems are compliant.

6. ISO 9000 applies to all organizational systems whether their output is a tangible product or a service. It is therefore as pertinent to governmental as to private operations.

7. When the ISO series is adopted by government buying organizations as their primary basis for supplier qualification under government solicitation practices, the issue of quality in products and services acquired for government use would be met in substantially all cases, allowing the government's preferred mechanism for securing competition to be used without applying the comprehensive auditing operations that currently impede economical and efficient government buying.

Government Perception and Regulation of Purchasing

Government purchasing at the federal level has earned a reputation for arbitrariness, for overspending, for delays, for waste, and for abuse. While this may overstate the case, the federal system has repeatedly shown a focus on process at the expense of results. This condition is brought about by the regulatory imperatives imposed by the Congress and by the responses of executive agencies to initiatives intended to improve purchasing. Regardless of perceptions, the federal system can produce good results as shown by many successful public acquisitions. There are current indications that change toward quality processes may lead to improvement. One improvement that may become feasible is the adoption of ISO 9000 as a qualification standard for suppliers and, possibly, as a qualification standard for internal agency operations. There are many other initiatives in process. The most current action is the proposed Federal Acquisition Streamlining Act of 1993 (FASA-93). This legislative proposal is a part of the administration's National Performance Review and draws upon recommendations that were proposed earlier, such as in the Section 800 Panel Report.**

---

*Comprehensive treatises dealing with ISO 9000 are found in two current books: Johnson, Perry L., *ISO 9000: Meeting the New International Standards*, (McGraw-Hill, New York, 1993); and Rabbitt, John T. and Bergh, Peter A., *The ISO 9000 Book: A Global Competitor's Guide to Compliance and Certification*, (Quality Resources, White Plains, NY, 1993).

**The DOD Advisory Panel on Streamlining and Codifying Acquisition Laws issued a report to the Congress on January 15, 1993. Known as the Section 800 Panel, the study was directed by the Congress in the FY 1991 Department of Defense Authorization Act.

Efforts to adopt commercial practices and to use commercial products are central in current proposals for changes in the federal acquisition process. These efforts have been discussed repeatedly since the Competition in Contracting Act (CICA) was passed in 1984, and some initiatives have been introduced. Purchases based on best-value evaluations and formal consideration of past performance as a factor in source selection are examples. The best-value concept and emphasis on evaluating past performance as part of source selection were proposed by the 1986 Packard Commission.*** Since then, important experimentation with the idea has been initiated in both defense and civilian procuring agencies. But efforts such as these are routinely challenged, based on the existing rules and preferences for ad hoc, price-competitive bidding for government contracts.

What is the likely outcome of this period of turmoil in federal procurement policy? How does it affect purchasers and purchasing throughout our economy? These are questions to which this conference might project answers.

It is unlikely that we could pinpoint specific policy changes, but I think we can postulate that a significant drag on productivity caused by excessive bureaucracy, complex procedures, and rules intended to protect or promote the interests of selected groups is being recognized by policy makers. Efforts to change are gaining ground and may be symbolized by the following summary of proposals contained in the FASA-93.

1. In an effort to reduce the effect of previously enacted encouragement of formal bid protests, the new proposal would

    a. provide earlier notices of contract award and expanded debriefing procedures;

    b. limit fees paid to attorneys, consultants, and expert witnesses in protest cases to $75.00 per hour;

    c. authorize dismissal and imposition of sanctions for frivolous protests and those brought in bad faith; and

    d. restrict GAO to recommend, not direct, payment of attorney fees in protest cases.

2. The act would establish a preference for procurement of commercial products and of nondevelopmental items.

3. The proposal would revise CICA to require evaluation factors and subfactors and their relative weights to be included in RFPs.

4. The procurement integrity law would be amended to streamline refusal provisions, consolidate revolving door rules, and revise certification provisions.

5. The act would raise the threshold for cost and pricing data requirements to $500,000.

6. The minimum wage requirements of the Walsh-Healey Act would be repealed.

7. Contracting under the 8(a) program directly by the procuring agency would be established by the act.

8. The act would establish a simplified, government-wide, acquisition threshold of $100,000, replacing the current $25,000 threshold.

If enacted, would this bill keynote any real change in the practical effect of government buying? Probably not in the short run. Probably so given a time horizon of five years. The catalog of proposals generated by the Section 800 panel contained a number of other key recommendations that would reduce administrative processes were not included in the proposed FASA-93. Nevertheless, some change in the perception of the effect of regulation seems to be emerging, and the trend is toward liberalization. These indications of change lead me to view the future of government purchasing positively. Changes at the federal level are in process, and are being influenced by the broadened scope of purchasing operations that is evident in the private sector.

***A *Quest For Excellence*, The President's Blue Ribbon Commission on Defense Management. (U. S. Government Printing Office, Washington, D. C., June 1986).

The Broadened Scope of Buyer Responsibilities

Strategic planning, customer orientation, early supplier involvement, partnership, and Just-in-Time systems dominate the recent literature of purchasing. These ideas draw purchasers toward a view of their work that is far different from the traditional heavy paperwork, reactive buying actions, and price-oriented competition for which the buying community is known. All of these concepts are derived from technology and information systems that enable purchasers to visualize and measure the effect of their decisions in a manner not feasible even one decade ago. The cumulative effect of these approaches to purchasing is overall improvement in product quality, reduced cost of operations, and increased competitiveness throughout the economy.

Within the private sector, the awakening of purchasing's potential for strategic involvement and the movement toward adoption of ISO 9000 promise major improvements in economic performance of forward moving companies and of the economy as a whole. It is my contention that ISO 9000, as a system designed to create reliable quality in organizations, should be adopted for application to internal operations of government as well as in industry. I do not think it too radical to propose quality registration of government agencies.

Within the buying community, the part most resistant to practicing the approaches discussed herein is the government buying system, especially at the federal level. This situation is rooted in the voluminous rule books and huge bureaucracies established to oversee the process. These oversight bureaucracies are made up of auditors, investigators, quality assurance, and contract administration organizations. The moves proposed in FASA-93, particularly the adoption of commercial practices and the raising of thresholds, hold promise for substantial change — even a metamorphosis — toward a more efficient and effective buying process within the government. It will, however, be slower to develop than equivalent improvement in the private sector.

GLOBAL CHANGES AND LOGISTICS RESPONSES

D. Clay Whybark, Ph.D.
University of North Carolina

Introduction

Great changes are taking place in the world of global business. Some truly multinational firms now operate facilities in virtually every corner of the globe. They make their sourcing, production, warehousing, and distribution decisions on a worldwide basis. When these business changes are coupled with the shifts in geopolitics and the emergence of new trade blocks, it is clear that the nature of international competition and trade has been unalterably changed. Moreover, global business will continue to evolve to an as yet undefined set of new patterns of trade and advanced organizational capabilities. These changes have already brought significant challenges and opportunities to logistics professionals, be they purchasing, physical distribution, logistics or materials managers.

In this article we review some of the recent changes and their effect on supply chains and the logistics environment. We document some of the barriers to implementing effective responses to the challenges and opportunities. We review some of the means by which manufacturing companies are responding to the changes, and draw some lessons for logistics professionals from the observations.

Global Changes

The rapid and pervasive changes in global competition, trade, and manufacturing have indelibly changed the face of international business. These changes have presented many challenges to logistics executives around the world and have simultaneously presented them with new opportunities (some wags would say "insurmountable opportunities"). For our purposes here, it is important to identify these changes and what their impact will be on global supply chains.

Changing Competition One of the most common reactions to the increase in global competition is, still, to look for ways to resist it, often with strong short-term justification. The opening of the economies of Eastern Europe provide a clear example. Many of the enterprises in the former centrally planned economies are not currently globally competitive. This has created severe disruptions in local economies, so much so that there are many people in those economies who want to return to the "good old socialist system."

Another type of reaction to the changing nature of competition is the creation of trade blocks in Western Europe, North America (NAFTA) and, perhaps, Southeast Asia. The creation of the European Union (formerly the European Economic Community) even led to the phrase "fortress Europe" in North America, a clear expression of concern for the changing face of economic trade. Nevertheless, some multinational companies have the ability to penetrate chinks in competitive barriers virtually wherever they occur in the world. Thus, some multinational companies have been accused of exporting jobs, dumping products and exploiting local populations, giving rise to the term "supernational" corporations. These reactions provide illustrations of the resistance to and concern for the changes taking place.

The negative view, however, obscures the advantages that come from wider and more open competition. The increased availability of both industrial and consumer products from all corners of the earth is a great source of information. Consumer products expand our understanding of our own market and what is being provided in other parts of the world. They provide ideas for new products for our local market and possible modifications to current products to cater to the tastes in other parts of the world. Global products that compete in our local market may open up niche opportunities for complimentary products as well.

Industrial products are great sources of ideas for new processes that improve product cost, quality, and/or desirability. Industrial products also provide insights into the manufacturing capability of global competitors and the logistics competence required to deliver them to our doorsteps. Products that are accepted by the world market also provide clear evidence of the increasing levels of global standards required to be competitive and are important elements for benchmarking requirements in the marketplace.

Increased awareness of the management practices of globally successful firms is another aspect of the information available through increased global competition. This is perhaps the most important aspect for management. The practices of superior producers provide us with a real demonstration of what is possible. Without actually seeing it happen, the concept of a lot size of one seems merely a theoretical dream. Without actually getting deliveries on a just-in-time basis from halfway around the world, it seems impossible. Without actually receiving products with rejects measured in parts per million, such levels of quality seem unattainable. That these things are happening shows us the global standards that must be met and the proof that it is possible to meet them.

To benefit from the knowledge that is available on products, processes and practices, the organization must be configured to capture and use the information. Moreover, logistics managers throughout the supply chain must be open to new concepts and be willing to share the information. This is often very difficult [14].

- A European car manufacturer had to send three teams to Japan before management would believe the reported levels of quality and cost that the Japanese car makers were achieving.

- Occasionally producers have taken their competitors to court for dumping products, only to find out that the low prices were not only covering the manufacturing and logistics costs required to sell in remote markets, but were providing profits as well.

- Some commodity manufacturers have even learned that some customers really want more than just the raw commodity at low cost. A sugar manufacturer added to profits and helped reduce a customer's costs by packaging sugar in a non-standard container. This added to the cost of production and distribution, but the price the customer was willing to pay for the new package more than compensated for the increased costs.

Changing Supply Chains In addition to international competition and the changes it has brought about, there also have been profound changes in the way that global businesses are being operated. In many companies, locating value-adding facilities is now based on evaluating their entire global logistics network. This analysis involves a comprehensive assessment of labor, tax, marketing, logistics, and other strategic trade-offs as opposed to simply focusing on costs. As a result, many companies' supply chains now cross oceans and country borders in a variety of previously unimaginable ways.

- Many companies are now using the software engineering capability of the Indian subcontinent to perform software maintenance and development. This enables North American firms, for example, to test software in their daytime and have the Indian firm make changes during their day [12].

- In the automotive industry, there are any number of countries that might be represented in the final product. This multinational participation has led some to question what is an American or European car [13].

- Pharmaceutical companies often have products that cross oceans and international boundaries several times from acquisition of the raw material to final production, packaging and delivery to the customer [16].

To manage international flows of information and product, many changes have been made in the management of supply chains and continued evolution will be required. The computer has come to play an indispensable role in keeping track of materials, capacities and capabilities. This has replaced some middle management functions and has avoided the necessity of hiring large numbers of clerical staff. The increased level of dependence on computer software and procedures has put pressure on the logistics community for increased technical and computer capability.

Another aspect of the increasingly complicated global supply chain is the need for integration. To be competitive, logistical flows now require global matching of demand to capacity, within and between companies. Thus we find greater integration needs between manufacturing, transportation, and storage facilities in the supply chains, between producers and customers, and between producers and service providers. This integration requires a greater understanding of the logistics system in total and a greater breadth of vision than has ever been needed before. Again we see the need for different management talents and vision than served us in the past.

Changing Logistics Environment It is evident from the preceding discussion that the world in which the art of logistics is performed has been affected by the global changes taking place. In addition, technical changes are providing new tools and alternatives for logistics professionals. Among these are the increasing use of container shipping, intermodal exchanges, bar coding, electronic data interchange (EDI), modeling technology, and other new techniques. There are other tools on the horizon, like artificial intelligence, advanced telecommunications systems and organization software, that will have a marked impact on the management of global flows of material in the future.

The creation of trading blocks has opened completely new manufacturing and distribution alternatives for companies. Many firms have already adjusted their distribution patterns to take advantage of previously unavailable alternatives in the European Union, for example. Others are moving manufacturing and distribution capacity to be conveniently located for NAFTA. The actions to date, however, have mostly been motivated by the internal market potential of the trading block. But many opportunities to restructure the flows between trading blocks are also now possible. These new logistics patterns are only beginning to emerge, but will continue to do so as creative logistics professionals use the new trading blocks to better position their production and/or distribution to serve global markets.

Other changes involve new ways to think about and use traditional technology. For example, we have all been led to believe that it is not possible to use ship transportation to support just-in-time (JIT) manufacturing. It is said to be simply too slow and too unreliable. With the reorganization of the port of Singapore and the development of reliably scheduled trips across the Pacific, parts are now delivered from the Far East to North America within hours of need. What's more, the parts are packed in containers in the correct order for assembly onto vehicles [10].

The same sorts of schedules will be possible for the ports served by the new canal that links the Black Sea with Rotterdam. In order to maintain schedules, the arrivals and departures will be closely controlled by the port authorities using advanced information technology. Having this capability opens new logistics alternatives to support modern supply chain requirements

One of the more far-sighted recent developments has to do with air transportation. To date many large freight airports and parcel distribution facilities have been developed and this trend will continue. Beyond these investments in current technology, however, is the development of the global transpark, an industrial park and just-in-time airport combined [4]. A transpark receives materials and parts by air, adds value in the manufacturing facilities and then flies the converted product to the next destination for more value added or to the customer. Like the rail systems of the past, which moved the centers of commerce from the seacoast and rivers, global transparks can create new centers of manufacturing activity wherever they are located.

Figure 68
Use of Computers and Materials Management Techniques

	At least some use
Computers in Forecasting	20%
Computers in Planning and Scheduling	46%
EOQ	28%
MRP	42%
JIT	44%

Figure 69
Benefits from Using Computer and Materials Management Techniques

	Statistically Significant* Reductions in:				
	Raw Material	WIP	Finished Goods	Safety Stock	Lateness
Use of Computers in Forecasting		Yes			
Use of Computers in Planning and Scheduling					
Use of EOQ					
Use of MRP					
Use of JIT	Yes				Yes

*Kruskal-Wallis non-parametric test at 5%

Barriers to Effective Responses

There are many barriers to effectively responding to the challenges and opportunities inherent in the global changes. We, in North America at least, are not very internationally oriented and that in itself is a barrier to recognizing and responding to global change [5]. But the most insidious barriers may be related to our traditional models and our experience in implementing new technology and approaches, particularly when we look at enterprises on a worldwide basis. The activities of manufacturing and logistics are still largely efficiency- or cost-oriented, not value- or customer-oriented. In addition, the use and payoff from some of the technology currently available for managing material flows have been disappointing.

Manufacturing Industry Focus A large part of the manufacturing community around the globe is still focused primarily on efficiency and cost reduction. This has been the training and experience of operations managers for years and is even institutionalized in our accounting systems. In many parts of the world, the major theory upon which manufacturing is still based is economies of scale. Similarly, the primary concern of many distribution organizations is still low-cost transportation. This focus on scale has led to very large plants, big production runs, high volume transportation vehicles, vertical integration of organizations, and many staff groups to manage the complexity. As global competition increases, many manufacturing companies continue to pursue efficiency as the only response possible for them. To be successful, this approach imposes important requirements on the supply chain.

The pursuit of efficiency has lead many firms to automate manufacturing. A great deal of engineering talent has gone into the development of computer-based production equipment. This equipment ranges from numerically controlled machine tools and robots, to large-scale, multistage machines for producing complicated parts. These installations are often part of a computer-integrated manufacturing (CIM) project in the company. In response to the lack of flexibility that such systems often imply, engineers in some companies have turned their attention to flexible manufacturing systems (FMS). But automation only speaks to part of the competitive needs no matter how flexible it might be.

A theory that is related to scale economies (also found in the blood of operations managers) is that high utilization of the labor force and equipment is needed for efficiency. This has many implications. It requires high levels of raw material and work-in-process inventory so that the people and machines are never without work. It means long runs of products to minimize setups and to fill transportation equipment. It implies high levels of finished goods inventories to be able to cycle through the product line. Large numbers of warehouses near the customers may be needed to provide reasonably quick delivery service, since small shipments are not tolerated.

The focus on scale economies with its long runs and high inventories places heavy demands on logistics professionals to manage the flow and storage of materials. The sheer size and complexity of the supply chain mean that the computer is needed and great amounts of information are required. These demands spawned a series of computer-based approaches to materials management. In many of the approaches, existing applications of current practice, often not suited to the new needs, were simply computerized. The development of low-cost computer power, however, made possible the development of approaches, like material and distribution requirements planning (MRP and DRP) which accepted the complexity and incorporated it into the system.

Implementation Disappointments The application of and benefits from using the computer in planning and controlling materials are disappointing. McLaughlin, et al. [7], provided evidence of this in an analysis of data from more than 20 countries. The data, developed by the Global Manufacturing Research Group [17], comes from two industries, and the sample includes more than 400 companies from such diverse places as the People's Republic of China and North America.

Figure 68 provides a summary of the use of computers and techniques for materials management in the sample. One of the first observations is that less than half of the respondents use computers for forecasting and production planning. The picture improves a little when the use of materials management techniques is considered. About a quarter of the respondents say they use the economic order quantity (EOQ) concept (28%) although some are using the other techniques. About half say they have some use of MRP (42%) or JIT (44%). It does seem the advanced techniques, whether designed to help manage complex material flows or to facilitate just-in-time manufacturing, are being implemented around the world.

106

When the benefits of using these techniques are considered, the picture is quite disappointing, however. Only the use of computers in planning and scheduling and the use of JIT provided any benefits and those were limited. Figure 69 shows the results. Firms using the computer for planning and scheduling were able to reduce their work-in-process inventory below that of those firms not using the computer. The use of JIT provides statistically significant reductions in lateness and raw material inventories. No other technique or measure showed a benefit.

The observed reduction in raw material inventory on the part of firms using JIT may confirm what many suppliers have been saying all along. JIT simply means that the raw material inventory is shifted to the supplier.

In addition to the lack of benefits from implementing computer and material management techniques, there have been technical difficulties in implementing EDI in many firms. The issues of communication standards still lead to headaches in companies trying to implement integrated information systems. Difficulties in implementation and less-than-promised results have left many managers very gun shy about the next "silver bullet" to be offered by a vendor of logistics solutions.

This rather bleak picture of the barriers arising from out-of-date theories and implementation shortfalls is not true for all firms. Some have been able to overcome the barriers and develop progressive approaches to the challenges. They provide us with important models of responses that are being implemented today.

Promising Responses to the Global Changes

Many "world-class" companies are already applying a variety of new theories to manufacturing. All evidence points to an expansion of the approaches that will be tried in the future. Although the discussion here will be couched in terms of manufacturing, the changes in logistics required to support these new approaches to the market are also pervasive.

Lean Manufacturing When the Japanese began to produce products that were both low cost and high quality, the manufacturing world was caught off guard. The systems employed by the Japanese were, apparently, much simpler than those used elsewhere and the manufacturing units were much smaller in scale. The lesson that seemed to come from the Japanese competitive assault on the world was that their systems and general management practices were quite different from those being applied in the West.

The concept of "lean" manufacturing was developed to incorporate some of the observations coming from the early reports on the Japanese manufacturers [18]. One of the first discoveries to catch the attention of the West was that much lower levels of inventories were found in Japanese companies. They had smaller lot sizes, much less work-in-process, and finished goods that moved quickly to global customers. Another observation was high levels of quality. Higher quality meant lower levels of safety stock and more satisfied customers.

In response to these reports, a great deal of Western attention was initially focused on the Kanban system for production control and statistical quality control. The essence of the Japanese approach was much broader than that, however, being summed up in the concept of removal of waste. Any activity that does not add value to the product is considered waste and is removed if possible.

The lean manufacturing approach was pioneered in the automotive industry and built upon the notions of waste removal. Its application has tended to equalize the global competitiveness of companies in the industry.

Agile Manufacturing Another promising response to the global challenges is called agile manufacturing [9]. Agile manufacturing has a number of elements in common with lean manufacturing and builds upon some of the same principles. The common elements include low inventories, small lot sizes, and high quality. Agile manufacturers add high flexibility and delivery reliability to this list. These enable the company to do "mass customization," the process of realizing the cost benefits of mass production while producing highly individualized products.

Where the byword in lean manufacturing is waste reduction, in agile manufacturing it is speed. This means very rapid design and manufacturing with fast, reliable delivery. Agile manufacturers will respond quickly to shifts in markets, tastes, and innovations that can affect their businesses. A national organization (The Agile Manufacturing Research Forum) has been established in the United States to promote the concepts of agile manufacturing. In order to distinguish this approach to manufacturing from past approaches, it has also been referred to as "mass customization" [11]. Some examples are already in operation.

- A Canadian manufacturer of refrigerators, washing machines, dishwashers, and ranges has implemented three-day service. A customer orders a washing machine one day, it is manufactured to the customer's specifications the next day, and is delivered to the customer (sometimes directly to the house) on the third day.

- An American producer of cellular phones, pagers, and other electronic devices now starts production within hours of receiving the customer's order. All devices are made to the customer's requirements.

- Although not yet successful, a Japanese automobile manufacturing company has been attempting to manufacture and deliver a customer's car in three days.

These agile manufacturing examples contain clear messages for logistics professionals. One message is that customer orders, materials, and products are simply not around long enough to be managed by complicated information systems. There is simply not enough time to gather, check, enter and process the information, at least not in the ways currently used. Secondly, the demands on the distribution and supply system are quite different from traditional "economies of scale manufacturing." For example, at the Canadian appliance manufacturer, shipments in truckload or carload lots have been virtually eliminated. Products are rarely delivered to a warehouse. They are shipped one-by-one to the retailers or customer. This has increased the transportation cost and scheduling detail, but has greatly reduced inventories and increased customer satisfaction.

Agile manufacturing places new requirements for flexibility and speed on the supply chain and new ideas are needed to meet them. Already some firms use "milk runs," in which the manufacturer picks up parts from several suppliers and has designed equipment to handle efficiently many small lots from several companies, as opposed to large lots from one company. The materials management systems to support these milk runs are much more nimble than those of the past.

Customer-Driven Manufacturing Customer-driven manufacturing builds on the agile manufacturing concepts by explicitly incorporating customers' needs in the processes. Several global quality initiatives have given impetus to this approach. ISO 9000 certification programs, the Baldrige award, and the Deming award all look for mechanisms that incorporate customers' requirements into the product design, production and distribution processes. Methods like quality function deployment are being used to do this in many total quality management (TQM) programs today [6].

The customer-driven manufacturing firm finds many ways to be involved with the customer. Often they have design teams, improvement groups, and other communication activities in which the customers are involved. Similarly, they are a part of such groups with their suppliers. The assignment of full-time representatives to reside with important customers is another way to "live with the customer" and learn their needs. In turn, there may be full-time representatives assigned to suppliers to assure that important needs are communicated along the supply chain. There are a variety of examples of customer-driven manufacturing firms, although the concepts are still fairly new [15].

- For some time now, some automotive and other equipment manufacturing firms have had their suppliers design parts to perform a specific function, as opposed to producing parts to the customer's specification. With high quality, these parts are delivered to the line in small lots for assembly directly onto the final product. A European car manufacturer has recently proposed to go a step further, however, and have the supplier actually mount the part on the final product.

- One of the Baldrige award winners in the United States is a sand and gravel producer. Even this company is customer-driven. By understanding their customers, mostly construction firms, they can save both time and costs, thereby improving their customers' profits and their own.

- Several examples of customer-driven manufacturing are being developed in Japan. Among these is a cosmetics firm that will home deliver an individually compounded formula, and a bicycle company that produces individual bicycles. Both of these firms deliver in less than two weeks [8].

Developing the organizations that can be customer driven requires substantial changes in the way we think about the company. The traditional geographical and functional organizational units simply are not up to the task [3]. The means for incorporating customer requirements into the company's processes and being rapidly responsive to them crosses functions, suppliers, and geography. Many companies are starting to reengineer their organizations and business processes to make them more responsive. This reengineering activity can span an entire supply chain of the firm [2].

Lessons Learned

A significant requirement for logistics professionals is to shed the models of the past. Notions of scale economies, the use of automation, and the role of inventories must be redirected to responsiveness, flexibility and speed. Some evidence of what can be gained by so doing can be gleaned from some of the examples cited here. Some lessons for reaching the customer-driven state can be drawn as well.

Responsiveness and Simplicity One of the lessons that can be drawn from customer driven-companies is that being responsive to customers often requires rebuilding the manufacturing and materials systems to achieve high levels of flexibility and speed. A key principle in the rebuilding process is simplification. Simplification of systems, procedures, set-ups, and approvals can all lead to improvements in flexibility and speed by reducing lead times and inventory. These reductions, in turn, provide opportunities to simplify or eliminate other activities that were once considered essential. For instance, many firms no longer take physical inventories nor do they expect invoices for material received. They assume that material was received because finished products were built and they simply pay for the material on the basis of the number of final products. Other firms are eliminating their computer systems for shop floor control and are using simple visual systems instead. Other forms of simplification are not only being developed, they will be required as global pressures for responsiveness continue.

A customer focus provides a unifying theme for deciding how to simplify. Whether the customer is inside or outside the firm, guidelines for designing or redesigning processes are determined by whether they increase value for the customer. The value to customers is the yardstick for determining if there is waste to be eliminated. Of course this means processes to evaluate that what is of value to the customer must be in place. Integration with the customer is a clear lesson here, but integration requirements are broader than just determining the customer needs.

Integration and Involvement Integration along the supply chain is an obvious requirement of customer-driven manufacturing. Customer needs must be assessed and then must be passed through the organization and onto suppliers. Geographical, functional, traditional, and legal barriers make this difficult, but it is already being done by some advanced firms. This integration spans the value satisfaction process from design to delivery and follow-up services. Providing this integration requires new mandates and forms of organization plus the involvement of all members of the supply chain.

Mixed customer-supplier teams have been in existence for a while. To be successful, they need more decision-making authority than what is thought possible in traditional firms. Moreover, their focus needs to be on problem solving rather than on following procedures, in order to respond to emerging needs and opportunities. This requires different motivation, training, and rewards from what has been typical in the past.

Conclusions

The argument here is simple: changes in the international business arena have already been pervasive and will continue. Not only does this bring us evidence of what is possible, it shows us what is necessary to compete globally. Many barriers to responding to the challenges exist, and the requirements for improvements in performance sometimes seem impossible to achieve. Some of the existing responses, however, provide models of what is possible and indications of what is required. Simplifying and focusing activities while integrating along the supply chain seem a daunting task. Nevertheless, the fact that some firms are meeting the challenges means that choosing not to change is no longer an option.

The mandate for change has clear implications for the logistics professional. Perhaps the most difficult is recognizing when an old assumption is blocking progress. When does the model need to change? When one realizes that the model must change, he or she will also need the management skills to design and implement the new system. Developing highly responsive supply, manufacturing, and distribution systems, as well as the management systems that support them, requires a high level of competence. Developing that competence is both the opportunity and the challenge facing logistics professionals today.

REFERENCES

1. Fogarty, D.W., J.H. Blackstone and T.R. Hoffman, *Production and Inventory Management, 2nd ed.*, Chapter 19, Southwestern, Cincinnati, 1991.

2. Fox, M.L., "Reengineer Your Supply Chain Planning," *APICS*, pp. 53-54, April 1993.

3. Giffi, C., A.V. Roth, G.M. Seal, *Competing in World-Class Manufacturing*, Irwin, Homewood, Il., 1990.

4. Kasarda, J.D., "Global Air CargoIndustrial Complexes as Development Tools," *Economic Development Quarterly*, Vol. 5, No. 3, August 1991.

5. Klassen, R. and D.C. Whybark, "Barriers to the Management of International Operations," *Journal of Operations Management*, Vol. 11, No. 4, 1993.

6. Long, J.B., "TQM: Stop Talking and Start Doing," *APICS*, pp. 29-32, April 1993.

7. McLaughlin C.P., G. Vastag and D.C. Whybark, "Statistical Inventory Control in Theory and Practice," *International Journal of Production Economics*, Vol. 35, Nos. 1-3, May 1994.

8. Murakoshi, T., "Customer Driven Manufacturing in Japan," *International Journal of Production Economics*, special issue on the coordination of sales and production edited by J. Wijngaard and D.C. Whybark, (forthcoming) 1994.

9. Nagel, R. and R. Dove, *21st Century Manufacturing Enterprise Strategy, Vols. I and II*, Iacocca Institute, Bethlehem, PA, 1991.

10. Pentimonti, E. "JIT Shipping," *OM Review*, Vol. 8, No. 1, pp 13-15, 1990.

11. Pine II, B.J., B. Victor and A.C. Boynton, "Making Mass Customization Work," *Harvard Business Review*, Sept./Oct. 1993.

12. Ramadorai, S. "Global Software Operations," *OM Review*, Vol. 8, No. 1, pp 19-22, 1990.

13. Reich, R. "Who Is Us?" *Harvard Business Review*, Jan./Feb. 1990.

14. Strebel, P. *Ford of Europe* (IMEDE Case G321) and "How Ford of Europe Reduced Its Financial Staff Headcount," *International Management*, pp 120-128, Oct. 1985.

15. Wallace, T.F. *Customer Driven Strategy*, Oliver Wight, Essex Junction, VT, 1992.

16. Wheeldon, C. "Manufacturing Logistics in Europe in the 1990's," PMA Materials Management Annual Technical Spring Symposium, San Diego, 1992.

17. Whybark, D.C. and G. Vastag, *Global Manufacturing Practices: A Worldwide Survey of Practices in Production Planning and Control*, Elsevier, Amsterdam, 1993.

18. Womack, J.P., D.T. Jones and D. Roos, *The Machine That Changed the World*, HarperCollins, New York, 1990.

APPENDIX E: DATA SYNTHESIS AND PRESCRIPTION •

At times, the level of analysis used by the investigators was sophisticated and rigorous. We can understand why an individual might have a hard time grasping exactly what specific analyses were performed. Nonetheless, the analysis was scientifically rigorous and correct. This last section of the report will reiterate the major findings from each of the previous analysis sections in simpler, concise language and provide a synthesis of those findings into salient future directions for our field.

Factor analysis is a technique for analyzing the underlying structure of a set of variables, in this case individual responses. The basic idea is that the members of a set of variables, each of which has been measured for a number of observations, have some of their structure determined by certain underlying common constructs or factors. Exploratory factor analysis requires that the investigators hypothesize beforehand the number of common criteria or factors. The hypothesis regarding the number of criteria (factors) must be based upon the nature of the considered variables and expectation of which factor is likely to load on which variable. This requirement was satisfied in the investigation by defining the major criteria and the stated sub-components of the criteria in the survey questionnaire. As mentioned previously, this subsequent survey instrument incorporating the major criteria was mailed to potential respondents. The investigators wished to use the survey responses to validate the hypothesized criteria and sub-components and to revise the model of purchasing's future options and roles.

The initial step in the exploratory factor analysis involves a mathematical technique called principal components analysis to determine the minimum number of factors that can adequately account for the observed variation in responses. The resulting number of eigenvalues greater than unity (one) indicates that a certain number of factors should be extracted from the data. This result should be consistent with the investigators hypothesized model of major criteria and their interaction.

Figure 70 shows the 36 scale items that were used in the exploratory factor analysis and their means, standard deviations, and definitions. Figure 71 shows the correlations among the 36 variables. The Bartlett test of sphericity was used to test the statistical significance of the observed correlations among the variables. The null hypothesis being that the observed correlation matrix is not different from an identity matrix (no correlation between scale items). The large value of the Bartlett statistic (3241.7997) and the associated significance probability (.00000) indicate that the null hypothesis is to be rejected and that the observed correlations are indeed statistically significant. Without such significance the exploratory factor analysis could not proceed.

The Kaiser-Meyer-Olkin measure of sampling adequacy is an index that measures how well the correlations between pairs of variables can be explained by other variables in the analysis. The Kaiser-Meyer-Olkin value of .91209 was adequate to justify further analysis of data.

FIGURE 70
RESPONSE VARIABLES (Q12): VARIABLE MEANS, STANDARD DEVIATIONS, AND DEFINITIONS

Analysis number 1   Listwise deletion of cases with missing values

	Mean	**Std Dev**	**Label**
Q12A	5.26224	1.15181	Use of Sourcing Teams
Q12AA	4.81173	1.13233	Shift from Cost Reduction to Avoidance
Q12AB	5.17704	1.01766	Purchasing Process Reengineering
Q12AC	4.77959	.91567	Integration of Purchasing and Design Engineering
Q12AD	5.04031	1.04737	Integration of Purchasing and Logistics
Q12AE	5.61735	.94565	Increased Use of Information Technology
Q12AF	4.12449	.97713	Third-Party Purchasing
Q12AG	5.42194	.97037	Reducing Purchasing Cycle Time
Q12AH	4.96837	1.20329	Use of "Alliance Purchasing"
Q12AI	5.14592	1.09039	"World-Class" Benchmarks
Q12AJ	4.58010	.94931	Reverse Logistics
Q12B	4.63520	.97288	Co-location of Supplier and Buying Firms
Q12C	5.29847	1.08304	Supply-base Reduction
Q12D	5.41276	1.01223	Increasing Technical Qualifications of Purchasing Employees
Q12E	5.57245	1.02064	Total Quality Management (TQM)
Q12F	5.53724	1.10759	Strategic Sourcing Management
Q12G	5.63112	1.00026	Purchasing Systems and Services
Q12H	5.39184	1.03554	Forecasting Material and Service Needs
Q12I	5.49949	.94427	Using Supplier Technical and Design Support
Q12J	5.65357	.95113	Reducing Purchasing Transaction Costs
Q12K	5.72245	1.02832	Electronic Data Interchange (Suppliers)
Q12L	5.69337	.99584	Strategic Supplier Alliances
Q12M	5.23724	1.15172	Supply Chain Intergration
Q12N	4.94082	1.05712	Increased Outsourcing
Q12O	4.65102	1.02694	Flattening the Purchasing Organization
Q12P	5.19286	1.10014	Cross-Functional Teams for Material Planning
Q12Q	5.35306	1.02449	Purchasing Performance Measurement Systems
Q12R	5.14949	1.04374	Just-in-Time Deliveries
Q12S	5.14490	1.00650	Environmentally Sensitive Purchasing
Q12T	5.49184	.95232	Total Cost (TCO) for Purchase Decisions
Q12U	4.73061	.98391	Supplier Councils
Q12V	4.76071	1.06132	Cooperative Network of Suppliers
Q12W	4.90459	1.12059	Global Sourcing
Q12X	5.05663	.93161	Time-based Purchasing Strategies
Q12Y	5.28520	.94159	Strategic Cost Management
Q12Z	5.24694	.99189	Organization Emphasis on Purchasing and Supply

Number of Cases =   196

Figure 71
RESPONSE VARIABLES (Q12): CORRELATION MATRIX

	Q12A	Q12B	Q12C	Q12D	Q12E	Q12F	Q12G	Q12H	Q12I	Q12J	Q12K	Q12L	Q12M	Q12N
Q12A	1													
Q12B	0.48176	1												
Q12C	0.4836	0.43185	1											
Q12D	0.37064	0.24393	0.29219	1										
Q12E	0.34216	0.18123	0.13213	0.39586	1									
Q12F	0.48051	0.3461	0.38245	0.44518	0.41359	1								
Q12G	0.34216	0.33745	0.23583	0.41356	0.43576	0.42703	1							
Q12H	0.1982	0.15615	0.04256	0.37036	0.38072	0.25248	0.44271	1						
Q12I	0.358	0.29582	0.37849	0.34499	0.29834	0.47265	0.25004	0.31199	1					
Q12J	0.29475	0.16499	0.2815	0.23445	0.31247	0.24948	0.37524	0.31321	0.40115	1				
Q12K	0.22153	0.26263	0.28519	0.23404	0.36788	0.29373	0.50207	0.30444	0.25943	0.4824	1			
Q12L	0.39009	0.3813	0.48346	0.29795	0.3522	0.42829	0.29557	0.19996	0.36457	0.34061	0.41214	1		
Q12M	0.41664	0.37906	0.4397	0.25107	0.35429	0.46761	0.30539	0.21159	0.45709	0.40236	0.42939	0.60486	1	
Q12N	0.25697	0.2879	0.17815	0.24839	0.23784	0.26613	0.25763	0.24583	0.15671	0.18979	0.24649	0.27651	0.43916	1
Q12O	0.30746	0.25781	0.28931	0.31081	0.22	0.26933	0.26139	0.16503	0.23975	0.27492	0.32291	0.24063	0.39299	0.44688
Q12P	0.59891	0.27665	0.2782	0.40828	0.39452	0.36119	0.35783	0.43695	0.35168	0.33485	0.31564	0.31128	0.39884	0.28176
Q12Q	0.52334	0.36769	0.28533	0.44732	0.46183	0.43957	0.45142	0.43251	0.3412	0.4994	0.47016	0.37497	0.38578	0.28551
Q12R	0.28796	0.19382	0.32171	0.18982	0.2883	0.30227	0.27173	0.22039	0.31285	0.37834	0.33433	0.35432	0.45565	0.17696
Q12S	0.28904	0.26872	0.14581	0.18754	0.15566	0.23977	0.33194	0.29916	0.18041	0.30747	0.25429	0.07249	0.24173	0.24547
Q12T	0.46593	0.31692	0.32825	0.34117	0.31871	0.37106	0.30175	0.3017	0.30413	0.32779	0.34434	0.32239	0.37545	0.18489
Q12U	0.32009	0.29915	0.19514	0.2428	0.35126	0.39541	0.28859	0.26298	0.33611	0.30401	0.34164	0.2754	0.4271	0.16219
Q12V	0.35314	0.37121	0.24622	0.26015	0.32873	0.39802	0.30766	0.26283	0.41636	0.27866	0.37155	0.37065	0.48514	0.19689
Q12W	0.24584	0.30819	0.25066	0.13499	0.07122	0.32359	0.12221	0.12885	0.23888	0.18337	0.18593	0.29722	0.34683	0.20811
Q12X	0.44426	0.2833	0.28741	0.35293	0.37163	0.39867	0.38184	0.35419	0.37785	0.36429	0.36139	0.23284	0.36256	0.23472
Q12Y	0.45275	0.27891	0.34998	0.35483	0.36953	0.49575	0.34374	0.31249	0.42058	0.38654	0.41335	0.34346	0.47604	0.23152
Q12Z	0.57261	0.3352	0.35753	0.41486	0.36368	0.43639	0.45131	0.34233	0.39803	0.44496	0.37061	0.39676	0.47754	0.29274
Q12AA	0.17649	0.0614	0.088	0.23118	0.26022	0.09431	0.2832	0.27587	0.22389	0.22383	0.27125	0.17939	0.19573	0.16218
Q12AB	0.50506	0.36822	0.45674	0.26528	0.22201	0.26032	0.47815	0.15666	0.24905	0.38603	0.48309	0.35877	0.42524	0.31607
Q12AC	0.26669	0.24362	0.12904	0.13573	0.18755	0.31572	0.23166	0.19879	0.30182	0.16584	0.18081	0.22841	0.27119	0.19074
Q12AD	0.27397	0.22502	0.20426	0.33265	0.18017	0.26067	0.30459	0.4223	0.29143	0.27869	0.27522	0.27377	0.3613	0.19735
Q12AE	0.40348	0.31889	0.26585	0.36525	0.30107	0.30617	0.48877	0.35379	0.31478	0.35491	0.50829	0.34521	0.40434	0.26994
Q12AF	0.18614	0.18504	0.1143	0.12495	0.13617	0.03891	0.16287	0.05909	0.06582	0.06755	0.17328	0.14325	0.31675	0.33111
Q12AG	0.36468	0.20717	0.30276	0.36795	0.28385	0.2181	0.39434	0.2948	0.2686	0.45023	0.40602	0.36988	0.39201	0.21839
Q12AH	0.39256	0.34317	0.39772	0.22441	0.20293	0.35308	0.25825	0.15186	0.30206	0.26751	0.28513	0.47721	0.46655	0.19272
Q12AI	0.55732	0.40149	0.33634	0.30198	0.346	0.36031	0.34187	0.28087	0.31385	0.30676	0.28506	0.34074	0.39539	0.33284
Q12AJ	0.24769	0.1669	0.10621	0.18529	0.13763	0.20014	0.26977	0.23646	0.18775	0.15436	0.17686	0.05535	0.22906	0.19975

	Q12O	Q12P	Q12Q	Q12R	Q12S	Q12T	Q12U	Q12V	Q12W	Q12X	Q12Y	Q12Z	Q12AA	Q12AB
Q12O	1													
Q12P	0.37839	1												
Q12Q	0.31039	0.61358	1											
Q12R	0.2646	0.35679	0.30442	1										
Q12S	0.12642	0.32948	0.33337	0.33836	1									
Q12T	0.29586	0.44924	0.47198	0.30631	0.41395	1								
Q12U	0.17461	0.22453	0.34346	0.13175	0.26441	0.41233	1							
Q12V	0.23297	0.34796	0.3999	0.23555	0.22897	0.38093	0.65539	1						
Q12W	0.15826	0.17208	0.27307	0.14432	0.16887	0.23238	0.28773	0.38258	1					
Q12X	0.32045	0.45577	0.44903	0.40072	0.32558	0.37746	0.31408	0.33898	0.23745	1				
Q12Y	0.31957	0.49748	0.45604	0.33236	0.35784	0.5064	0.41193	0.47527	0.3012	0.62293	1			
Q12Z	0.31969	0.56214	0.55533	0.28252	0.34142	0.4382	0.3117	0.36395	0.19935	0.54686	0.59101	1		
Q12AA	0.16266	0.30425	0.26824	0.17789	0.20665	0.25823	0.17666	0.15925	0.01451	0.29003	0.31035	0.33766	1	
Q12AB	0.34005	0.41036	0.42291	0.27961	0.30757	0.34952	0.20106	0.19155	0.19099	0.31944	0.32782	0.44734	0.24701	1
Q12AC	0.19177	0.24986	0.26913	0.19563	0.16737	0.28221	0.29321	0.31642	0.24069	0.33489	0.39251	0.29625	0.18135	0.34312
Q12AD	0.19399	0.36694	0.30673	0.19688	0.30256	0.25334	0.30474	0.33484	0.20774	0.29806	0.37932	0.28472	0.21459	0.38737
Q12AE	0.26063	0.40235	0.41234	0.22841	0.28576	0.36739	0.36418	0.36965	0.30964	0.31449	0.43926	0.37063	0.3703	0.56863
Q12AF	0.29598	0.17061	0.04552	0.15076	0.12824	0.23135	0.23679	0.22371	0.10654	0.1384	0.23589	0.05907	0.21494	0.23692
Q12AG	0.38416	0.4701	0.47376	0.39467	0.27748	0.31085	0.19368	0.25848	0.20968	0.39072	0.3315	0.44936	0.26943	0.4075
Q12AH	0.30161	0.29517	0.3647	0.27671	0.19994	0.28256	0.25378	0.40789	0.17996	0.20495	0.32655	0.32333	0.11729	0.35621
Q12AI	0.21584	0.43034	0.52504	0.22735	0.35048	0.40829	0.38032	0.36844	0.32841	0.34041	0.3553	0.44024	0.18559	0.42299
Q12AJ	0.09794	0.26006	0.24169	0.17951	0.42494	0.2367	0.26924	0.25514	0.11713	0.29005	0.28308	0.20398	0.24267	0.26191

	Q12AC	Q12AD	Q12AE	Q12AF	Q12AG	Q12AH	Q12AI	Q12AJ
Q12AC	1							
Q12AD	0.45147	1						
Q12AE	0.35634	0.53414	1					
Q12AF	0.14018	0.18699	0.28169	1				
Q12AG	0.22496	0.26191	0.42319	0.23968	1			
Q12AH	0.27671	0.35653	0.39023	0.27662	0.36293	1		
Q12AI	0.29622	0.2818	0.42837	0.19079	0.34679	0.37219	1	
Q12AJ	0.16265	0.32049	0.32183	0.30338	0.25238	0.25619	0.40302	1

Kaiser-Meyer-Olkin Measure of Sampling Adequacy = .91209
Bartlett Test of Sphericity = 3241.7997, Significance = .00000

After ascertaining the statistical significance of the correlation matrix, the next step was to do an exploratory factor analysis to see if the 36 scale items (variables) could be condensed into a smaller set of independent factors. This is what the investigators mean by dimensionality reduction. Figure 72 shows the result of the principal components analysis, which is the first step in factor analysis. It can be seen from Figure 72 that the first eight factors have eigenvalues greater than unity (one). These together explain 61.1 percent of the variation in the data (see the cumulative percentage, cum pct, column). Figure 73 shows the initial factor loadings, that is, the correlation of the variables with the eight factors extracted. The standard procedure at this stage is to establish a cutoff point of, say, 0.40, and to treat all correlations or factor loadings below this cutoff value to be essentially zero. Although there is no precise standard value for a cutoff point that is prescribed by the factor analysis procedure, values in the range 0.3 to 0.4 have been used in past research. Applying this procedure to Figure 73 values, it can be seen that many of the factor loadings will be retained as significant.

FIGURE 72
RESPONSE VARIABLES (Q12): PRINCIPAL COMPONENTS ANALYSIS INITIAL STATISTICS

Extraction   1 for analysis   1, Principal Components Analysis (PC)

Initial Statistics:

Variable	Communality	* *	Factor	Eigenvalue	Pct of Var	Cum Pct
Q12A	1.00000	*	1	12.05253	33.5	33.5
Q12AA	1.00000	*	2	1.90119	5.3	38.8
Q12AB	1.00000	*	3	1.63397	4.5	43.3
Q12AC	1.00000	*	4	1.59037	4.4	47.7
Q12AD	1.00000	*	5	1.33487	3.7	51.4
Q12AE	1.00000	*	6	1.21555	3.4	54.8
Q12AF	1.00000	*	7	1.17445	3.3	58.1
Q12AG	1.00000	*	8	1.09139	3.0	61.1
Q12AH	1.00000	*	9	.98608	2.7	63.8
Q12AI	1.00000	*	10	.95402	2.7	66.5
Q12AJ	1.00000	*	11	.87524	2.4	68.9
Q12B	1.00000	*	12	.80151	2.2	71.1
Q12C	1.00000	*	13	.78834	2.2	73.3
Q12D	1.00000	*	14	.72716	2.0	75.4
Q12E	1.00000	*	15	.71929	2.0	77.3
Q12F	1.00000	*	16	.64913	1.8	79.2
Q12G	1.00000	*	17	.63386	1.8	80.9
Q12H	1.00000	*	18	.60064	1.7	82.6
Q12I	1.00000	*	19	.54040	1.5	84.1
Q12J	1.00000	*	20	.51935	1.4	85.5
Q12K	1.00000	*	21	.49716	1.4	86.9
Q12L	1.00000	*	22	.46252	1.3	88.2
Q12M	1.00000	*	23	.43323	1.2	89.4
Q12N	1.00000	*	24	.40429	1.1	90.5
Q12O	1.00000	*	25	.39090	1.1	91.6
Q12P	1.00000	*	26	.37258	1.0	92.6
Q12Q	1.00000	*	27	.35287	1.0	93.6
Q12R	1.00000	*	28	.33164	.9	94.5
Q12S	1.00000	*	29	.31835	.9	95.4
Q12T	1.00000	*	30	.30001	.8	96.3
Q12U	1.00000	*	31	.27559	.8	97.0
Q12V	1.00000	*	32	.24933	.7	97.7
Q12W	1.00000	*	33	.21766	.6	98.3
Q12X	1.00000	*	34	.21267	.6	98.9
Q12Y	1.00000	*	35	.20398	.6	99.5
Q12Z	1.00000	*	36	.18789	.5	100.0

PC   extracted   8 factors.

FIGURE 73
RESPONSE VARIABLES (Q12): FACTOR MATRIX

Factor Matrix:

	Factor 1	Factor 2	Factor 3	Factor 4	Factor 5	Factor 6	Factor 7	Factor 8
Q12Q	.72413	.16592	-.22702	-.04159	-.12112	-.03047	-.11643	-.16761
Q12Z	.71549	.10526	-.26034	-.01121	-.17476	-.00158	.04649	.09296
Q12Y	.71101	.05283	-.01965	-.21253	.00479	.05593	.25709	.21817
Q12M	.70284	-.33542	.03027	.08841	.24045	.09582	.15629	-.00492
Q12A	.68734	-.16590	-.12560	.01511	-.45143	.03250	-.06320	.03121
Q12P	.68435	.21327	-.15530	.06283	-.23943	.11237	.01500	.14896
Q12AE	.66902	.11174	.29313	.09961	.12489	-.24643	-.27287	.04497
Q12AI	.64409	-.06535	.13377	-.06318	-.32728	-.01355	-.11238	-.22786
Q12X	.64300	.19490	-.13698	-.11936	-.09602	.08284	.27840	.19175
Q12AB	.63259	-.04027	.11274	.40854	-.13386	-.30077	-.16674	.00990
Q12T	.62925	.03818	.00802	-.11791	-.15868	.05592	.18721	-.08671
Q12F	.62875	-.19941	-.22512	-.30172	-.03938	.13233	-.10107	.03890
Q12G	.62019	.28013	-.04569	.09425	.08009	-.06799	-.29593	-.21997
Q12V	.61097	-.20330	.17252	-.41849	.23159	.08052	.05612	-.13291
Q12K	.60841	.10625	-.03808	.19146	.39221	-.18172	-.01854	-.28517
Q12AG	.60740	.13767	-.07844	.34274	.06342	-.08730	.09954	.00463
Q12L	.59780	-.39277	-.19810	.11091	.26321	-.07280	-.11335	-.02366
Q12J	.57923	.14521	-.21286	.11903	.24212	-.26691	.21103	-.17441
Q12I	.57569	-.12817	-.18605	-.24562	.13006	-.04967	.10118	.22042
Q12AH	.55720	-.32666	.14402	.13150	.05497	-.13179	-.05107	.06024
Q12D	.55306	.17058	-.21443	-.03856	-.07352	.23133	-.33149	.12144
Q12U	.55167	-.09387	.23410	-.46776	.21612	.09316	.03182	-.24525
Q12E	.54706	.21484	-.25068	-.13072	.21564	.28979	-.15968	-.15989
Q12AD	.54235	.12401	.34182	-.09331	.09405	-.27414	-.20454	.36129
Q12B	.53451	-.36793	.06676	-.01043	-.25774	-.00151	-.18575	-.17402
Q12C	.52872	-.46555	-.20551	.20081	-.15805	-.16878	.03974	.03859
Q12R	.50695	-.00468	-.17564	.19558	.12131	-.07691	.48316	.01093
Q12H	.50092	.48075	-.03457	-.17930	.12162	.04697	-.19369	.00739
Q12O	.49580	-.09628	-.02702	.37521	.07468	.40198	.04064	.17438
Q12S	.48258	.27686	.23036	-.03959	-.31456	-.13421	.32398	-.25893
Q12W	.40477	-.35215	.14424	-.24456	-.00066	-.06887	.01913	-.06949
Q12AA	.39759	.41128	.10643	.11940	.14134	.03706	.06073	.17745
Q12AF	.32175	-.08130	.56229	.29668	.12418	.39451	.11837	.01926
Q12AJ	.41683	.23076	.49752	-.04261	-.24268	-.01143	.16243	-.13304
Q12N	.45384	-.06630	.18980	.28765	-.00662	.48207	-.12013	-.03960
Q12AC	.46496	-.04608	.25140	-.20785	.03389	-.17267	-.06606	.48692

As mentioned previously, the initial step in the exploratory factor analysis involved principal components analysis to determine the minimum number of factors that can adequately account for the observed variation in responses. The resulting number of eigenvalues greater than one indicated that eight factors were extracted from the data. Rotation of the factor matrix grouped the variables into eight factors with no clear differentiation of sub-components. This result violated the empirical specification that there should be at least three variables **clearly loading** on each factor. When variables load highly on several factors interpretation becomes difficult. Based on the pattern of factor loadings we concluded that interpretability of these factors was poor.

In order to improve the interpretability of the factors, several **rotation** methods were tried. First, the **quartimax** rotation method was performed. Most of the variables load highly on Factor 1 leaving very few significant loadings on factors 2 through 7. Next, the **oblimin** rotation, an oblique rotation method, was performed. The pattern of loadings did not permit meaningful interpretation of the factors. Finally, the **varimax** rotation method, which preserves the orthogonality of the factors, was implemented. Figure 74 shows the resulting factor loadings for the variables. The resulting pattern of factor loadings affords meaningful interpretation of the eight factors. The factor loadings with a value of .4000 or above (printed in boldface type) were used to characterize the factor interpretations

FIGURE 74
RESPONSE VARIABLES (Q12): FACTOR MATRIX-VARIMAX ROTATION

VARIMAX   rotation   1 for extraction   1 in analysis 1 - Kaiser Normalization.

VARIMAX converged in 29 iterations.

Rotated Factor Matrix:

	Factor 1	Factor 2	Factor 3	Factor 4	Factor 5	Factor 6	Factor 7	Factor 8
Q12C	**.68168**	-.05038	.27474	.26141	.09726	.05462	-.08040	.07372
Q12A	**.66102**	.29557	.35378	-.00613	.08814	.08683	.22489	.10183
Q12B	**.63964**	.14355	-.00283	.03339	.28351	.05517	.15457	.13668
Q12AB	**.53088**	.15833	.03236	.42390	-.12137	.36862	.21699	.17988
Q12AI	**.50529**	.29899	.07345	.07199	.24728	.09626	.42004	.10351
Q12L	**.45915**	.14435	.14270	.42207	.32848	.11587	-.27298	.15865
Q12AH	**.44688**	-.01624	.09561	.26899	.24381	.30007	.01714	.22494
Q12E	.01000	**.64390**	.18071	.21602	.28940	-.06748	-.03425	.15297
Q12D	.23438	**.64194**	.21403	-.00526	.04913	.15427	-.04679	.15725
Q12H	-.12678	**.62562**	.14463	.16289	.13497	.25666	.17586	.00256
Q12G	.19347	**.58656**	-.03645	.39575	.08991	.17284	.19289	.08051
Q12Q	.35244	**.56062**	.25713	.28805	.15411	.05239	.21935	-.01420
Q12X	.09873	.29350	**.63298**	.13609	.14525	.14894	.22042	.08873
Q12Y	.13337	.22235	**.59648**	.13808	.33611	.26095	.18055	.12240
Q12R	.10882	-.04234	**.52771**	.49906	.08105	-.03145	.11250	.13758
Q12Z	.35272	.41872	**.49684**	.20381	.07397	.12468	.14781	.03560
Q12P	.28844	.45997	**.47270**	.11092	-.03376	.16120	.22131	.16621
Q12I	.20053	.18229	**.46975**	.16005	.36660	.23289	-.10843	-.02967
Q12T	.25174	.23404	.37293	.14500	.27096	.04572	.34233	.10629
Q12K	.10310	.29311	.01349	**.70850**	.23110	.11370	.08600	.12515
Q12J	.10127	.20704	.29099	**.66503**	.14060	.05089	.12349	-.05672
Q12AG	.21603	.23008	.28411	**.50003**	-.07054	.15494	.14867	.22724
Q12U	.04739	.21936	.06570	.10989	**.75211**	.11526	.22601	.08077
Q12V	.13691	.16971	.16408	.13468	**.74474**	.16025	.11966	.11489
Q12W	.32998	-.04337	.07975	.03968	**.48217**	.13928	.08454	.02577
Q12M	.33602	.04633	.30566	.38387	**.43539**	.12130	-.03778	.38095
Q12F	.38557	.37786	.34198	.00415	**.43441**	.07095	-.06992	.02350
Q12AD	.11182	.18509	.09930	.12704	.16035	**.75443**	.14192	.06054
Q12AC	.13670	.04815	.27484	-.04578	.22545	**.66686**	.02816	.04668
Q12AE	.24544	.30634	-.05222	.36351	.16341	**.56663**	.21352	.16250
Q12AA	-.18221	.28902	.24079	.23967	-.06472	.30568	.18327	.21441
Q12S	.11881	.10209	.23604	.19953	.09707	.03539	**.72276**	.00145
Q12AJ	.04896	.06821	.06566	.03556	.14501	.22187	**.67615**	.19849
Q12AF	-.00983	-.08842	-.02086	.06785	.16086	.15995	.23673	**.76112**
Q12N	.21490	.26795	.03303	.03855	.08799	.00640	.08800	**.66444**
Q12O	.21351	.19097	.30304	.16521	-.01441	.04260	-.09445	**.61943**

The eight factors and their interpretations are as follows.

- Factor 1 - **Supply Chain Management**.

The scale items that load highly on this factor are supply base reduction, the use of sourcing teams, co-location of buyer and supplier, purchasing process re-engineering, the use of "World-Class" benchmarks, the implementation of supplier strategic alliances, and an emphasis by purchasing on implementing alliance purchasing agreements.

- Factor 2 - **Total Quality Purchasing Management**

The items that load highly on this factor are the use of total quality management (TQM) principles within purchasing, increasing the technical qualifications of purchasing employees, forecasting both material and service needs, a focus by purchasing on internal systems and services, and an increasing emphasis on purchasing perform-ance measurement systems.

- Factor 3 - **Time-Based Purchasing**

The items that load highly on this factor are use of time-based purchasing strategies, strategic cost management, just-in-time deliveries, an organizational emphasis on purchasing and supply management, the use of cross-func-tional teams, and using supplier technical and design support.

- Factor 4 - **Transaction Cost Management**

The items that load highly on this factor are the use of electronic data interchange (EDI) with suppliers, an emphasis on reducing purchasing transaction costs, and a thrust to reduce purchasing cycle time.

- Factor 5 - **External Organization Integration**

The items that load highly on this factor are the use of supplier councils, the development of a cooperative network of suppliers, increased global sourcing activity, supply chain integration, and strategic sourcing manage-ment.

- Factor 6 - **Internal Organizational Integration**

The items that load highly on this factor are the strategic integration of the purchasing and logistics functions, the strategic integration of the purchasing and design engineering functions, and an increased use of information technology by purchasing.

- Factor 7 - **"Green" Purchasing**

The items that load highly on this factor are environmentally sensitive purchasing, and reverse logistics, that is, the role of logistics in recycling, reuse, waste disposal, and management of hazardous materials, and the movement of used materials "backward" up the supply chain from the customer to suppliers.

- Factor 8 - **Outsourcing**

The items that load highly on this factor are an increased use of third-party purchasing, an increased outsourcing of material and service needs, and a flattening of the purchasing organization.

Prior to developing a "bivariate correlation-based" descriptive model that relates the 8 previously calculated purchasing futures factors to the various strategic competitive priorities stressed by the survey respondent firms, such measures of competitive strategic priority needed to be calculated from the survey data. Toward this goal, 12 competitive priorities (the responses to survey questions 11A through 11L), were factor analyzed in order to reduce them to a logical set of strategic composite factors to be used in the descriptive bi-variate correlation phase of the analysis. Again, these 12 variable were taken from responses provided to questions found in the survey instrument. Figure 75 presents the means, standard deviations, number of valid observations, and descriptions of these variables. Figure 76 shows the correlations among the twelve variables. The Bartlett test of sphericity was used to test the statistical significance of the observed correlations among the variables, the null hypothesis being that the observed correlation matrix is not different from an identity matrix (no correlation between scale items). The large value of the Bartlett statistic (957.67373) and the associated significance probability (.00000) indicate that the null hypothesis is to be rejected and that the observed correlations are statistically significant. Without such significance the factor analysis should not proceed.

FIGURE 75
RESPONSE VARIABLES (Q11): INITIAL STATISTICS
- - - - - - — - — - - - - - - - - - - - - - - - - F A C T O R A N A L Y S I S -
Analysis number 1   Listwise deletion of cases with missing values

	Mean	Std Dev	Label
Q11A	5.45420	1.21291	Product/Service Innovation
Q11B	4.87304	1.26785	Low Prices
Q11C	4.07913	1.42189	Rapid Volume Changes
Q11D	6.17855	.84479	High Quality
Q11E	5.72116	1.10761	High Performance
Q11F	5.32667	1.33440	Fast Deliveries
Q11G	5.99913	.92578	Dependable Delivery
Q11H	6.08116	.84580	Customer Service
Q11I	5.34319	1.24670	Technology Leadership
Q11J	4.94348	1.24857	Customization
Q11K	4.70725	1.38185	Environmental Concerns
Q11L	4.91536	1.29367	Process Innovation

Number of Cases =   345

FIGURE 76
RESPONSE VARIABLES (Q11): CORRELATION MATRIX

Correlation Matrix:

	Q11A	Q11B	Q11C	Q11D	Q11E	Q11F	Q11G	Q11H	Q11I	Q11J	Q11K	Q11L
Q11A	1.00000											
Q11B	-.05557	1.00000										
Q11C	.13643	.17547	1.00000									
Q11D	.34450	.02603	.13607	1.00000								
Q11E	.38810	-.06093	-.00123	.51012	1.00000							
Q11F	.12803	.11954	.34974	.24884	.26140	1.00000						
Q11G	.15372	.19725	.14728	.41089	.40009	.55378	1.000					
Q11H	.28680	.01696	.09046	.37963	.37450	.24204	.45439	1.00000				
Q11I	.41638	-.00809	.10379	.25782	.35924	.01065	.05879	.11800	1.00000			
Q11J	.31073	.08505	.11443	.24047	.31531	.19353	.27049	.33455	.30757	1.00000		
Q11K	-.02403	.10252	.15775	.02389	.08890	.11154	.16445	.10349	.24076	.12758	1.00000	
Q11L	.27266	.08185	.24173	.23371	.24367	.11498	.23074	.15933	.38799	.27532	.41218	1.00000

Kaiser-Meyer-Olkin Measure of Sampling Adequacy = .75288

Bartlett Test of Sphericity = 957.67373, Significance =   .00000

118

The Kaiser-Meyer-Olkin measure of sampling adequacy is an index that measures how well the correlations between pairs of variables can be explained by other variables in the analysis. The Kaiser-Meyer-Olkin value of .75288 was adequate to justify further analysis of data. The initial factor analysis statistics are provided in Figure 77. Figure 78 shows the initial factor loadings, i.e., the correlation of the variables with the 8 factors extracted. It can be seen in the Figure 78 values that too many of the factor loadings will be retained as significant. The resulting pattern of factor loadings affords meaningful interpretation of the four strategic priority factors. To solve this problem, the **varimax** rotation method, which preserves the orthogonality of the factors, was implemented. Figure 79 shows the resulting factor loadings for the variables. The resulting pattern of factor loadings affords meaningful interpretation of the four strategic priority factors. The factor loadings with a value of .4000 or above (printed in boldface type) were used to characterize the factor interpretations The four strategic competitive factors and their interpretations are as follows.

FIGURE 77
RESPONSE VARIABLES (Q11): PRINCIPAL COMPONENTS ANALYSIS INITIAL STATISTICS

Extraction   1 for analysis   1, Principal Components Analysis (PC)
Initial Statistics:

Variable	Communality	*	Factor	Eigenvalue	Pct of Var	Cum Pct
Q11A	1.00000	*	1	3.47720	29.0	29.0
Q11B	1.00000	*	2	1.52017	12.7	41.6
Q11C	1.00000	*	3	1.43492	12.0	53.6
Q11D	1.00000	*	4	.96371	8.0	61.6
Q11E	1.00000	*	5	.88998	7.4	69.0
Q11F	1.00000	*	6	.77109	6.4	75.5
Q11G	1.00000	*	7	.66402	5.5	81.0
Q11H	1.00000	*	8	.55954	4.7	85.7
Q11I	1.00000	*	9	.54343	4.5	90.2
Q11J	1.00000	*	10	.43450	3.6	93.8
Q11K	1.00000	*	11	.42049	3.5	97.3
Q11L	1.00000	*	12	.32095	2.7	100.0

PC   extracted   4 factors.

FIGURE 78
RESPONSE VARIABLES (Q11): FACTOR MATRIX AND FINAL STATISTICS

Factor Matrix:

	Factor 1	Factor 2	Factor 3	Factor 4
Q11E	.69247	-.24513	-.28658	-.14161
Q11G	.66468	.45340	-.24533	-.24186
Q11D	.66375	-.07773	-.30040	.04622
Q11H	.61073	.06602	-.32543	-.22000
Q11J	.58226	-.12406	.04403	.00236
Q11A	.57289	-.42934	-.07653	.41491
Q11F	.51911	.57471	-.15213	.13815
Q11I	.51659	-.51810	.35588	.10903
Q11B	.13278	.50301	.27232	.08685
Q11K	.31804	.10659	.65196	-.50026
Q11L	.55471	-.12590	.55585	-.10599
Q11C	.33510	.40674	.36151	.60204

Final Statistics:

Variable	Communality	*	Factor	Eigenvalue	Pct of Var	Cum Pct
Q11A	.69055	*	1	3.47720	29.0	29.0
Q11B	.35236	*	2	1.52017	12.7	41.6
Q11C	.77088	*	3	1.43492	12.0	53.6
Q11D	.53898	*	4	.96371	8.0	61.6
Q11E	.64178	*				
Q11F	.64200	*				
Q11G	.76605	*				
Q11H	.53165	*				
Q11I	.67383	*				
Q11J	.35636	*				
Q11K	.78782	*				
Q11L	.64376	*				

FIGURE 79
RESPONSE VARIABLES (Q11): FACTOR MATRIX — VARIMAX ROTATION

VARIMAX   rotation   1 for extraction   1 in analysis 1 - Kaiser Normalization.

VARIMAX converged in 9 iterations.

Rotated Factor Matrix:

	Factor 1	Factor 2	Factor 3	Factor 4
Q11G	**.81142**	-.08944	.27453	.15579
Q11H	**.71375**	.13111	-.03081	.06387
Q11E	**.65235**	.42453	-.17661	.06937
Q11D	**.61885**	.38890	.03702	-.05825
Q11A	.22679	**.78694**	.04299	-.13409
Q11I	.02836	**.73726**	-.06364	.35415
Q11J	.37539	**.41099**	.07248	.20315
Q11C	-.04268	.27503	**.83240**	.02285
Q11F	.56079	-.04722	**.56906**	-.03824
Q11B	.04515	-.16688	**.53236**	.19764
Q11K	.06940	-.02881	.09037	**.87978**
Q11L	.11288	.43052	.17238	**.64494**

120

- Factor 1 - **Total Quality Focus**.

The items that load highly on this strategic competitive priority are dependable delivery, customer service, high-performance products and/or services, and consistently high quality.

- Factor 2 - **Differentiation/Customization Focus**.

The items that load highly on this strategic competitive priority are product/service innovation, technology leadership, and product and service customization.

- Factor 3 - **The Traditional Purchasing Focus**.

The items that load highly on this strategic competitive priority are rapid volume changes, fast deliveries, and low prices.

- Factor 4 - **The Eco-Organization Focus**.

The items that load highly on this strategic competitive priority are environmental concerns, and process innovation.

One can interpret these four factors as strategic themes stressed by the respondents to the survey instrument. These factors are consistent with other competitive priorities written in the current literature and theorized in the papers presented during the academic symposium at Michigan State University.

Bivariate correlations coefficients were calculated using the eight previously defined future directions factors and the four previously defined strategic competitive priority factors. The resulting Bivariate correlation coefficients and their statistical significance levels are provided in Figure 80. The Bivariate correlations that are significant at the p < .06 level are shown in boldface type.

These correlation results are interesting and have important implications for purchasing's future role within the corporations. First, firms whose competitive directions are based upon a total quality competitive priority (dependable delivery, customer service, high-performance products and/or services, and consistently high quality) intend to stress as purchasing's future role in the corporation a total quality purchasing management focus (Factor 2-8), and transaction cost management focus (Factor 4-8). *By implication, this indicates that the purchasing function should focus on developing the activities of electronic data interchange (EDI) with suppliers, an emphasis on reducing purchasing transaction costs, a thrust to reduce purchasing cycle time, the use of total quality management (TQM) principles within purchasing, increasing the technical qualifications of purchasing employees, forecasting both material and service needs, a focus by purchasing on internal systems and services, and an increasing emphasis on purchasing performance measurement systems.*

Second, firms whose competitive directions are based upon a differentiation/customization competitive priority (product/service innovation, technology leadership, and product and service customization) intend to stress as purchasing's future role in the corporation a total quality purchasing management focus (Factor 2-8), time-based purchasing strategies (Factor 3-8), internal organizational integration (Factor 6-8), and environmentally sensitive, "green" purchasing (factor 7-8). By implication, this indicates that the purchasing function should focus on developing the use of total quality management (TQM) principles within purchasing, increasing the technical qualifications of purchasing employees, forecasting both material and service needs, a focus by purchasing on internal systems and services, an increasing emphasis on purchasing performance measurement systems, strategic cost management, Just-in-Time deliveries, an organizational emphasis on purchasing and supply management, the use of cross-functional teams, using supplier technical and design support, the strategic integration of the purchasing and logistics functions, the strategic integration of the purchasing and design engineering functions, an increased use of information technology by purchasing, environmentally sensitive purchasing, and reverse logistics, that is, the role of logistics in recycling, reuse, waste disposal, and management of hazardous materials and the movement of used materials "backward" up the supply chain from the customer to suppliers.

FIGURE 80
BIVARIATE CORRELATIONS OF FACTOR SCORES FOR Q11 INTO
FOUR FACTORS AND Q12 INTO EIGHT FACTORS

Bivariate correlations of Factor Scores - Question 11 into 4 factors versus Question 12 into 8 factors.

CORRELATION COEFFICIENTS

	FACTOR 1-4	*FACTOR 2-4*	*FACTOR 3-4*	*FACTOR 4-4*
FACTOR 1-8	0.1006	0.0028	-0.0843	0.1962
	191	191	191	191
	p=.166	p=.969	p=.246	**p=.007**
FACTOR 2-8	0.1596	0.1939	-0.0793	0.0482
	191	191	191	191
	p=.027	**p=.007**	p=.276	p=.508
FACTOR 3-8	0.0293	0.1942	0.1446	-0.0093
	191	191	191	191
	p=.687	**p=.007**	**p=.046**	p=.899
FACTOR 4-8	0.1951	0.0988	0.0658	0.2059
	191	191	191	191
	p=.007	p=.174	p=.365	**p=.004**
FACTOR 5-8	0.0522	0.0725	0.2274	0.0760
	191	191	191	191
	p=.473	p=.319	**p=.002**	p=.296
FACTOR 6-8	-0.0699	0.1968	-0.1131	0.0522
	191	191	191	191
	p=.337	**p=.006**	p=.119	p=.473
FACTOR 7-8	0.0706	-0.1608	-0.1377	0.3565
	191	191	191	191
	p=.332	**p=.026**	**p=.057**	**p=.000**
FACTOR 8-8	0.0217	0.1057	0.1150	0.0282
	191	191	191	191
	p=.766	p=.146	p=.133	p=.698

FACTOR 1-8: Supply Chain Management
FACTOR 2-8: Total Quality Purchasing Management
FACTOR 3-8: Time-Based Purchasing Strategies
FACTOR 4-8: Transaction Cost Management
FACTOR 5-8: External Organization Integration
FACTOR 6-8: Internal Organizational Integration
FACTOR 7-8: "Green" Purchasing
FACTOR 8-8: Outsourcing
FACTOR 1-4: Total Quality Focus
FACTOR 2-4: Differentiation Focus
FACTOR 3-4: Traditional Purchasing Focus
FACTOR 4-4: Eco-Organization Focus

Third, firms whose competitive directions are based upon a traditional competitive priority (rapid volume changes, fast deliveries, and low prices) intend to stress as purchasing's future role in the corporation time-based purchasing strategies (Factor 3-8), external organization integration (Factor 5-8), and environmentally sensitive, "green" purchasing (Factor 7-8). *By implication, this indicates that the purchasing function should focus on developing strategic cost management models, Just-in-Time deliveries, an organizational emphasis on purchasing and supply management, the use of cross-functional teams, using supplier technical and design support, the use of supplier councils, the development of a cooperative network of suppliers, increased global sourcing activity, supply chain integration, strategic sourcing management strategies, environmentally sensitive purchasing, and reverse logistics, that is, the role of logistics in recycling, reuse, waste disposal, and management of hazardous materials and the movement of used materials "backward" up the supply chain from the customer to suppliers.*

Fourth, firms whose competitive directions are based upon an eco-organization competitive priority (environmental concerns, and process innovation) intend to stress as purchasing's future role in the corporation supply chain management (Factor 1-8), transaction cost management (Factor 4-8), and environmentally sensitive, "green", purchasing (Factor 7-8). *By implication, this indicates that the purchasing function should focus on supply base reduction, the use of sourcing teams, co-location of buyer and supplier, purchasing process reengineering, the use of "World-Class" benchmarks, the implementation of supplier strategic alliances, an emphasis by purchasing on implementing alliance purchasing agreements, the use of electronic data interchange (EDI) with suppliers, an emphasis on reducing purchasing transaction costs, a thrust to reduce purchasing cycle time, environmentally sensitive purchasing, and reverse logistics, that is, the role of logistics in recycling, reuse, waste disposal,and management of hazardous materials, and the movement of used materials "backward" up the supply chain from the customer to suppliers.*

Finally, irrespective of the strategic direction of the firms that responded to the questionnaire, outsourcing (Factor 8-8: an increased use of third-party purchasing, an increased outsourcing of material and service needs, and a flattening of the purchasing organization), was not one of their primary strategic focuses for purchasing. This result is not surprising and substantiates the finding from previous phases of the research that documented that third-party purchasing was not a popular component of any strategic purchasing factors and that further flattening of the purchasing organization was not extremely likely.

A MANUFACTURING VERSUS NONMANUFACTURING INDUSTRY COMPARISON

In order to increase the relevance to the varied industry readers of this report, an additional analysis similar to the one used above was applied to two subgroups of respondents: manufacturing and nonmanufacturing. Each survey respondent provided a listing of the major products and services produced by his or her business unit. This product/service was used to classify the responses into two mutually exclusive groups, manufacturing and nonmanufacturing. When these separate groups were factor analyzed, the eight strategic purchasing factors uncovered were the same for both groups and analogous to those mentioned previously. The major difference occurred in the determination of the strategic competitive factors. Where previously four strategic competitive factors were used in the entire group analysis, five strategic competitive factors were used for the subgroup analyses.

The five strategic competitive factors and their interpretations are as follows.

- Factor 1 - **Total Quality Focus**.

The items that load highly on this strategic competitive priority are dependable delivery, customer service, high performance products and/or services, and consistently high quality.

- Factor 2 - **Differentiation/Customization Focus**.

The items that load highly on this strategic competitive priority are product/service innovation, technology leadership, and product and service customization.

- Factor 3 - **The Traditional Purchasing Focus**.

The items that load highly on this strategic competitive priority are rapid volume changes, and fast deliveries.

- Factor 4 - **The Eco-Organization Focus**.

The items that load highly on this strategic competitive priority are environmental concerns, and process innovation.

- Factor 5 - **Cost Focus**.

The single item that load highly on this strategic competitive priority is providing customers with low prices.

One can interpret these five factors as strategic themes stressed by the manufacturing and nonmanufacturing respondents to the survey instrument. Once again, Bi-variate correlations coefficients were calculated using the eight previously defined future directions factors and the five previously defined strategic competitive priority factors. The resulting Bivariate correlation coefficients and their statistical significance levels for the separate manufacturing and nonmanufacturing industries are provided in Figures 81 and 82. The Bivariate correlations that are significant at the p ‹ .06 level are shown in boldface type.

FIGURE 81
BIVARIATE CORRELATIONS (MANUFACTURING) OF FACTOR SCORES FOR Q11 INTO
FIVE FACTORS AND Q12 INTO EIGHT FACTORS

Bivariate correlations of Factor Scores - Question 11 into 5 factors versus Question 12 into 8 factors.

CORRELATION COEFFICIENTS (Manufacturing)

	FACTOR1-5	*FACTOR2-5*	*FACTOR3-5*	*FACTOR4-5*	*FACTOR5-5*
FACTOR 1-8	0.0828	0.1653	0.1160	-.0328	-.0511
	138	138	138	138	138
	p=.334	**p=.053**	p=.175	p=.703	p=.552
FACTOR 2-8	-.0484	-.0604	0.2249	-.1489	0.0114
	138	138	138	138	138
	p=.573	p=.482	**p=.008**	p=.081	p=.894
FACTOR 3-8	0.2655	0.1021	0.0815	0.1290	0.1311
	138	138	138	138	138
	p=.002	p=.234	p=.342	p=.132	p=.125
FACTOR 4-8	0.0008	0.2414	0.0683	0.0247	0.0020
	138	138	138	138	138
	p=.993	**p=.004**	p=.426	p=.774	p=.981
FACTOR 5-8	-.0393	0.0862	0.1681	-.1697	-.0405
	138	138	138	138	138
	p=.647	p=.315	**p=.049**	**p=.047**	p=.637
FACTOR 6-8	0.0388	0.1049	0.0516	0.0985	-.0361
	138	138	138	138	138
	p=.651	p=.221	p=.548	p=.251	p=.674
FACTOR 7-8	0.1402	-.1204	0.1209	0.0256	-.0715
	138	138	138	138	138
	p=.101	p=.160	p=.158	p=.766	p=.405
FACTOR 8-8	-.0755	0.0742	0.0112	0.1709	0.1252
	138	138	138	138	138
	p=.379	p=.387	p=.897	**p=.045**	p=.143

FACTOR 1-8: Supply Chain Management
FACTOR 2-8: Total Quality Purchasing Management
FACTOR 3-8: Time-Based Purchasing Strategies
FACTOR 4-8: Transaction Cost Management
FACTOR 5-8: External Organization Integration
FACTOR 6-8: Internal Organizational Integration
FACTOR 7-8: "Green" Purchasing
FACTOR 8-8: Outsourcing
FACTOR 1-5: Total Quality Focus
FACTOR 2-5: Differentiation Focus
FACTOR 3-5: Traditional Purchasing Focus
FACTOR 4-5: Eco-Organization Focus
FACTOR 5-5: Price Minimization Focus

125

FIGURE 82
BIVARIATE CORRELATIONS (NONMANUFACTURING) OF FACTOR SCORES FOR Q11 INTO
FIVE FACTORS AND Q12 INTO EIGHT FACTORS

Bivariate corellations of Factor Scores - Question 11 into 5 factors versus Question 12 into 8 factors.

	CORRELATION COEFFICIENTS (NonManufacturing)				
	FACTOR 1-5	*FACTOR 2-5*	*FACTOR 3-5*	*FACTOR 4-5*	*FACTOR 5-5*
FACTOR 1-8	0.0345	0.1100	-.0359	0.1447	0.3788
	138	138	138	138	138
	p=.028	p=.438	p=.801	p=.306	p=.006
FACTOR 2-8	0.0876	0.4178	0.1317	0.3017	0.0583
	138	138	138	138	138
	p=.537	**p=.002**	p=.352	**p=.030**	p=.681
FACTOR 3-8	-.0403	0.1748	0.2248	-.0320	0.2207
	138	138	138	138	138
	p=.776	p=.215	p=.109	p=.822	p=.116
FACTOR 4-8	-.0373	0.1260	0.1119	0.1318	0.0750
	138	138	138	138	138
	p=.793	p=.373	p=.429	p=.352	p=.597
FACTOR 5-8	0.1196	0.1688	0.0490	0.1117	-.0301
	138	138	138	138	138
	p=.398	p=.232	p=.730	p=.430	p=.832
FACTOR 6-8	-.0133	0.2201	0.0698	-.0136	0.0063
	138	138	138	138	138
	p=.926	p=.117	p=.623	p=.924	p=.965
FACTOR 7-8	0.0571	0.2138	-.2485	-.1747	-.1240
	138	138	138	138	138
	p=.687	p=.128	p=.076	p=.216	p=.381
FACTOR 8-8	0.1214	0.0008	-.2583	0.5180	0.0447
	138	138	138	138	138
	p=.391	p=.995	p=.064	**p=.000**	p=.753

FACTOR 1-8: Supply Chain Management
FACTOR 2-8: Total Quality Purchasing Management
FACTOR 3-8: Time-Based Purchasing Strategies
FACTOR 4-8: Transaction Cost Management
FACTOR 5-8: External Organization Integration
FACTOR 6-8: Internal Organizational Integration
FACTOR 7-8: "Green" Purchasing
FACTOR 8-8: Outsourcing
FACTOR 1-5: Total Quality Focus
FACTOR 2-5: Differentiation Focus
FACTOR 3-5: Traditional Purchasing Focus
FACTOR 4-5: Eco-Organization Focus
FACTOR 5-5: Price Minimization Focus

These correlation results have important implications for purchasing's future role within the corporations. Our interpretation of the major differences between these two industry groups are as follows.

1. Environmentally sensitive, "green" purchasing is a distinct competitive direction in the nonmanufacturing industry group, but it is not a major factor in the manufacturing industry. *By implication, this suggests that the manufacturing industry has not yet wholeheartedly adopted environmentally sensitive manufacturing nor purchasing strategies within their business units. It seems that nonmanufacturing industries are further developed in this area.*

2. The correlations between strategic competitive directions and purchasing priorities are significantly higher in the nonmanufacturing industry than in the manufacturing industry. *By implication, this suggests that the nonmanufacturing industry has stronger feelings concerning which purchasing futures should be used to support certain competitive directions.*

3. An emphasis on integration both within the supply chain and within the business unit itself (an external organization integration and an internal organizational integration) is much stronger in the manufacturing industry than in the nonmanufacturing industry. *By implication, this suggests that the use of "virtual corporation" concepts is viewed as imperative for future competitive success by manufacturing companies.*

4. There is a much greater emphasis on supply chain integration and transaction-cost management strategies within the manufacturing industry than the nonmanufacturing industry. *By implication, this suggests that the cost reduction will remain an important future imperative for the manufacturing industry.*

Because this study was concerned primarily with the future directions of purchasing and materials management, the survey questions obviously concentrated heavily on these aspects of purchasing. Consequently, there is a small probability that the nature of the information supplied by the respondents could also have contributed to these results. In any case, the results are informative and interesting. Certainly, these findings merit further study and attention.

CENTER FOR ADVANCED PURCHASING STUDIES •

THE CENTER FOR ADVANCED PURCHASING STUDIES (CAPS) was established in November 1986 as the result of an affiliation agreement between the College of Business at Arizona State University and the National Association of Purchasing Management. It is located at The Arizona State University Research Park, 2055 East Centennial Circle, P.O. Box 22160, Tempe, Arizona 85285-2160 (Telephone [602] 752-2277).

The Center has three major goals to be accomplished through its research program:

to improve purchasing effectiveness and efficiency;
to improve overall purchasing capability;
to increase the competitiveness of U.S. companies in a global economy.

Research published includes 24 focus studies on purchasing/materials management topics ranging from purchasing organizational relationships to CEOs' expectations of the purchasing function, as well as benchmarking reports on purchasing performance in 26 industries.

Research under way includes: *Measuring Purchasing Effectiveness; Ethics in Purchasing Management: Issues, Helps, and Challenges; Purchasing Consortiums*; and the benchmarking reports of purchasing performance by industry.

CAPS, affiliated with two 501 (c) (3) educational organizations, is funded solely by tax-deductible contributions from organizations and individuals who want to make a difference in the state of purchasing and materials management knowledge. Policy guidance is provided by the Board of Trustees consisting of: